WILLIAM GILLOCK

Recital Collection

ISBN 978-1-4950-8028-9

WILLIS MUSIC

Exclusively Distributed By

HAL•LEONARD®

7777 W. Bluemound Rd. P.O. Box 13819 Milwaukee, WI 53213

Visit Hal Leonard Online at
www.halleonard.com

Preface

2017 marks William Gillock's centennial year. To celebrate, this newly selected compendium of Gillock's finest recital pieces was re-edited and re-engraved.

Gillock firmly believed that repertoire choice was crucial to a student's success. "If a piece seems worth the effort of learning, the student is more likely to give willingly the time and thought necessary for a beautiful performance," he advised in a 1979 letter to teacher Becky Corley.

Renowned pedagogue Lynn Freeman Olson famously observed that the Gillock name "spells magic to teachers around the world" and that in each of his compositions "musical quality comes first." Martha Hilley, professor at the University of Texas in Austin, opined similarly in a 1993 article: "As a composer he stood for all that is right in piano literature."

We agree. It is our hope that the music of William Gillock will continue to be performed for centuries to come. Happy 100th, Bill.

-The Publishers

Contents

To the Metairie Senior Music Club

Adagio Esotico

William Gillock

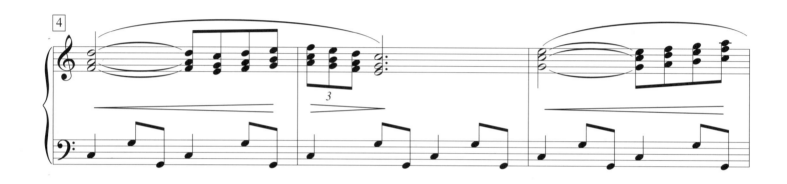

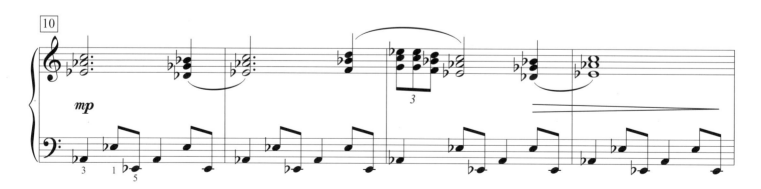

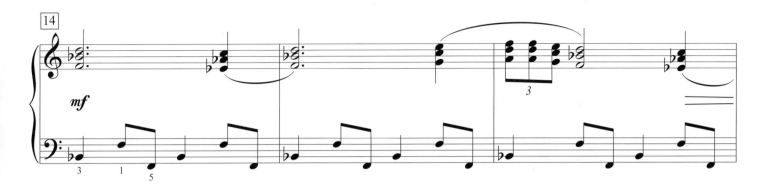

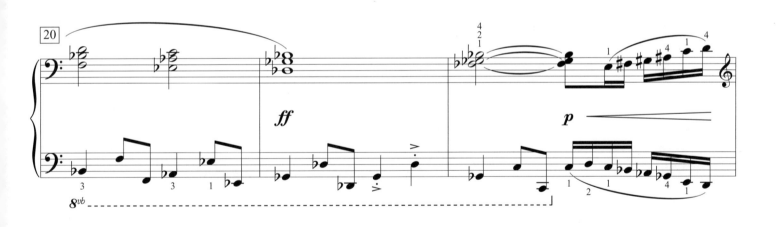

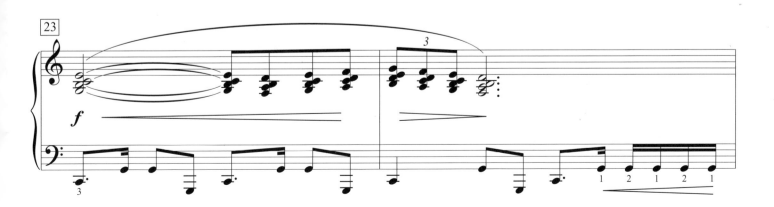

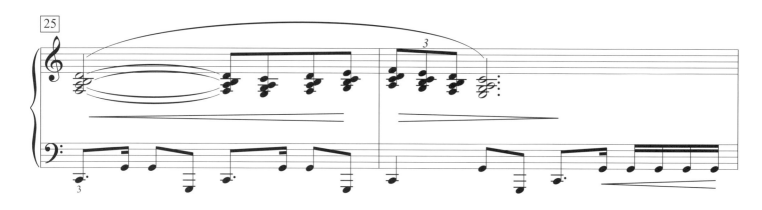

To Yvonne Reynolds

Arabesque Sentimentale

William Gillock

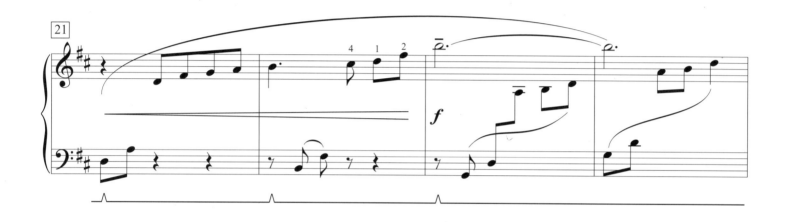

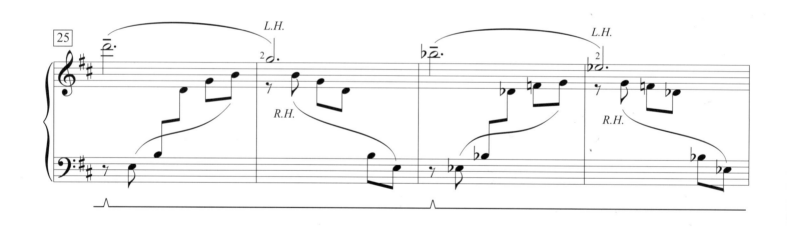

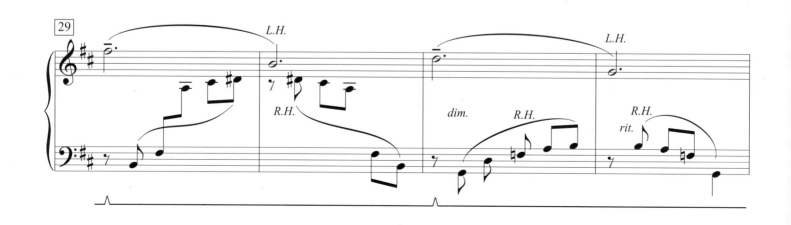

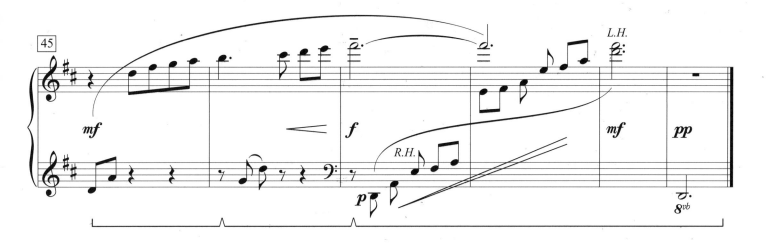

Barcarolle

William Gillock

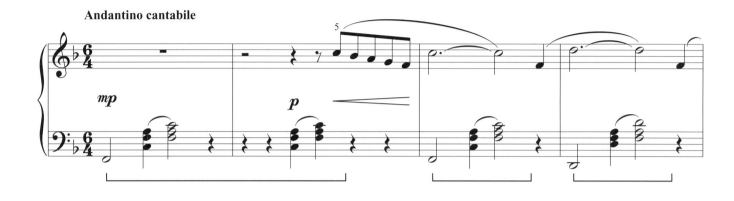

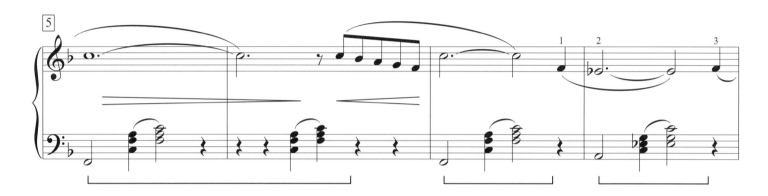

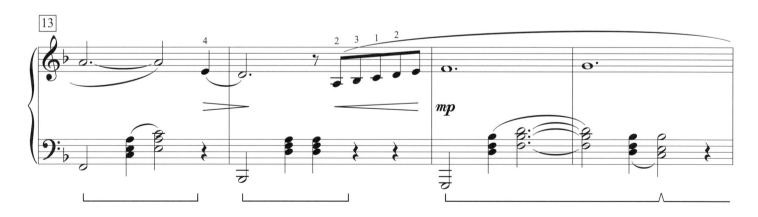

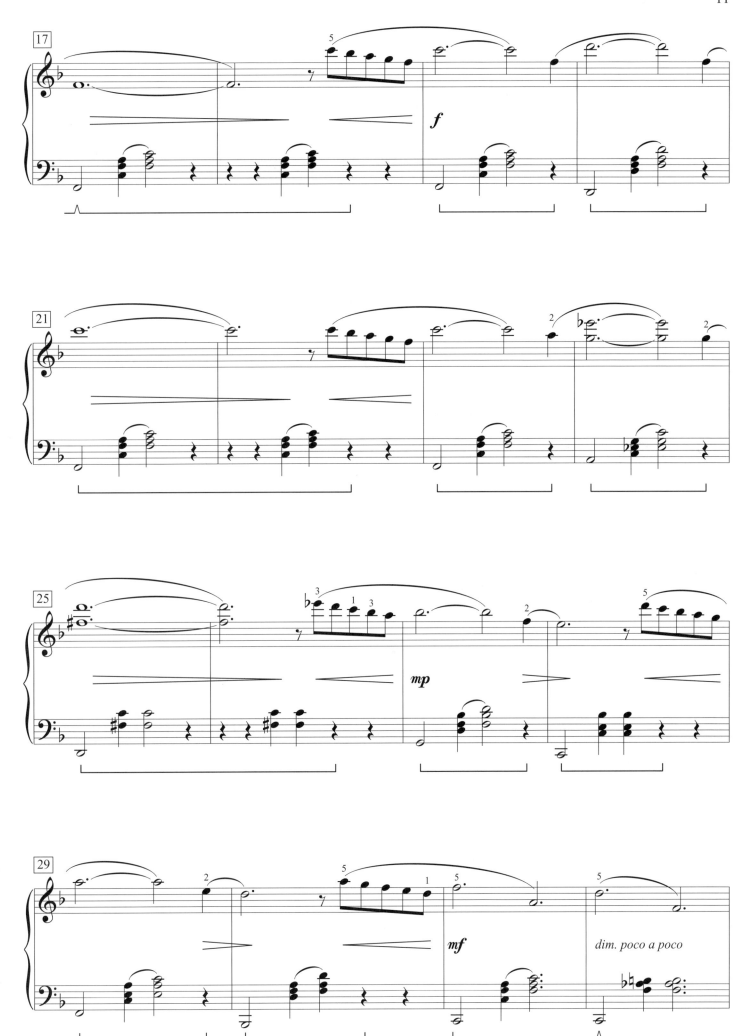

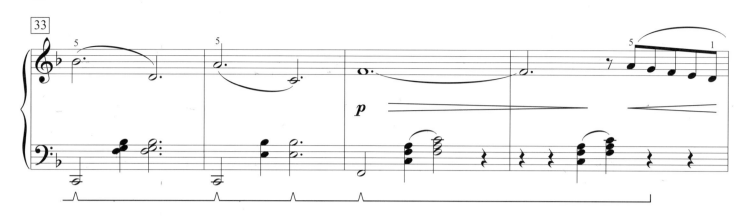

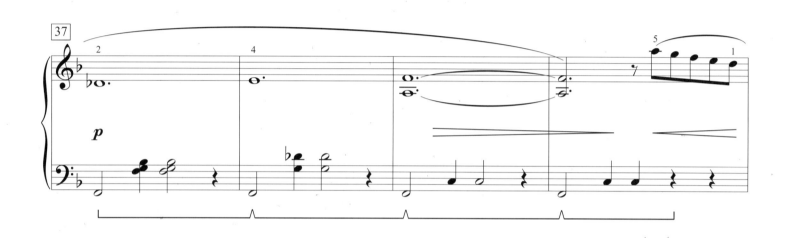

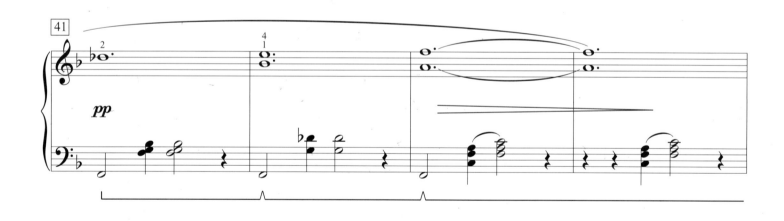

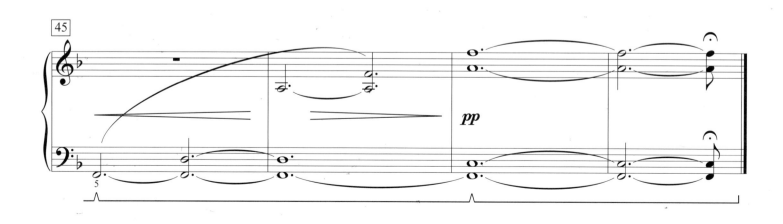

Bill Bailey
Won't You Please Come Home

Hughie Canon
Arranged by William Gillock

light staccato throughout, like a plucked string bass

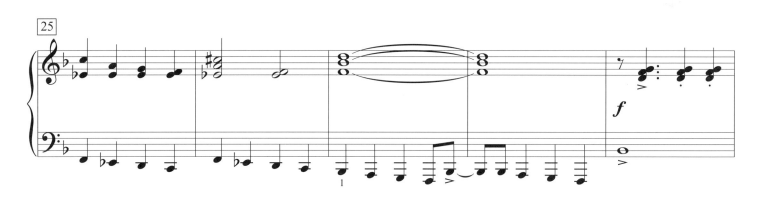

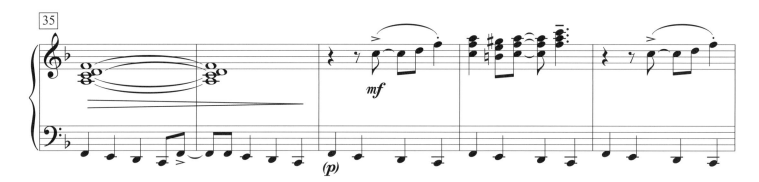

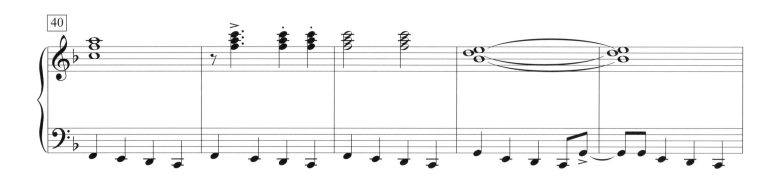

To Elizabeth Morris

Blue Mood

William Gillock

Moderately; with a precise beat

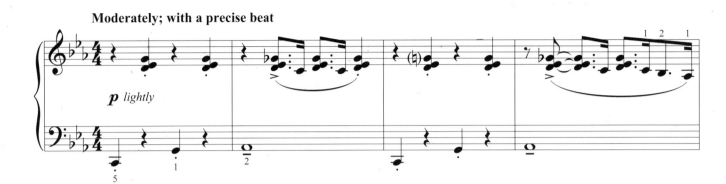

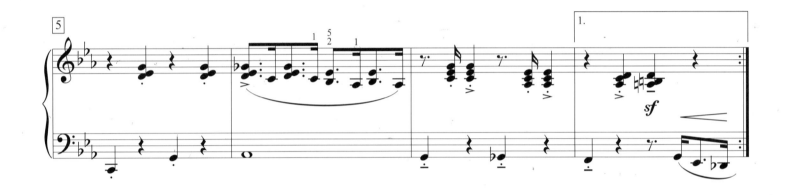

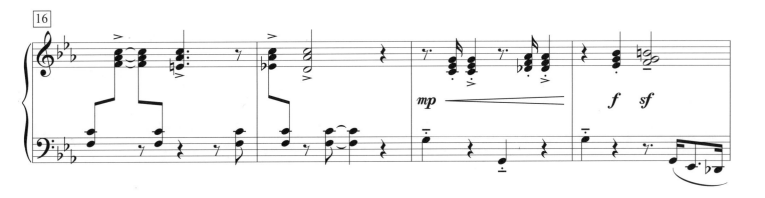

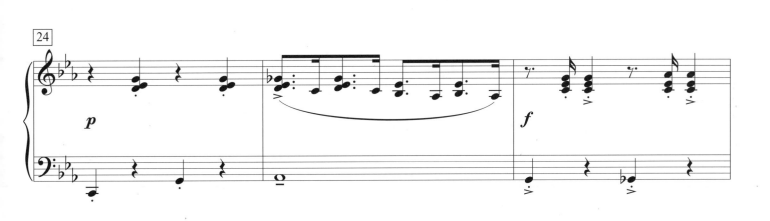

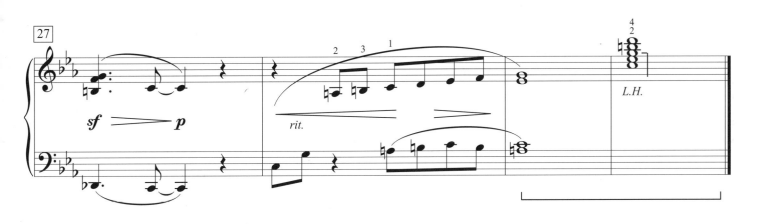

To Kimberly Diane

Blues Motif

William Gillock

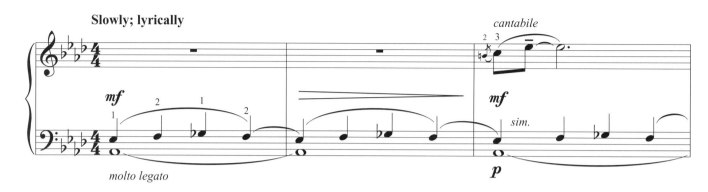

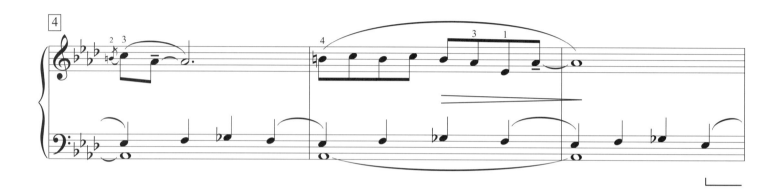

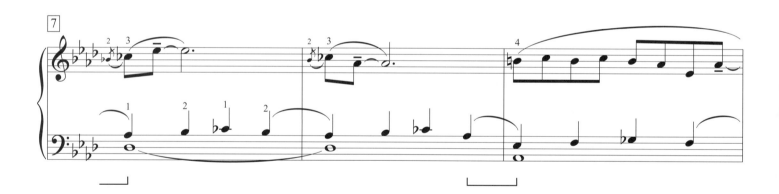

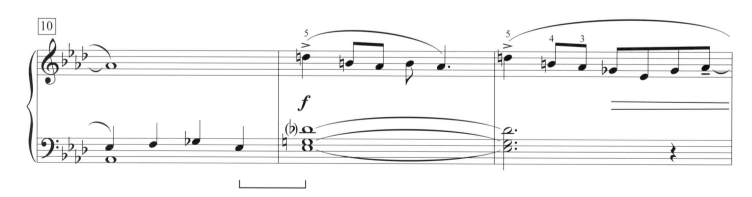

Note: Although the composer prefers that all eighth notes be played as written, the player may take the liberty of treating any or all as ♩♪ patterns.

To Douglas Kozuma

Blues Prelude

William Gillock

Slow ballad, with flexibility

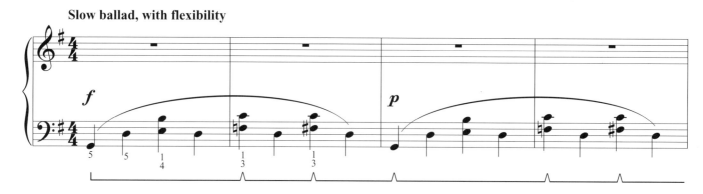

To my friend, Nina M. Stackpole

Castanets

William Gillock

* Shading and touches *simile* throughout.

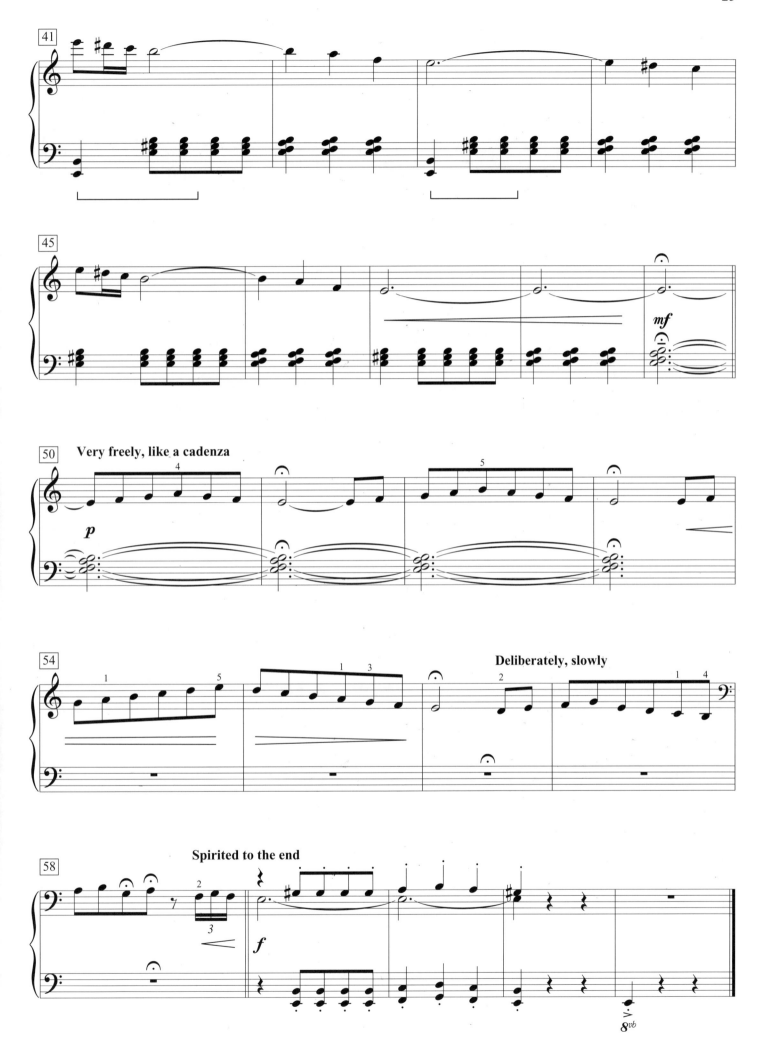

To Daryl Kamita

Boogie Prelude

William Gillock

Bourbon Street Saturday Night

William Gillock

Capriccietto

William Gillock

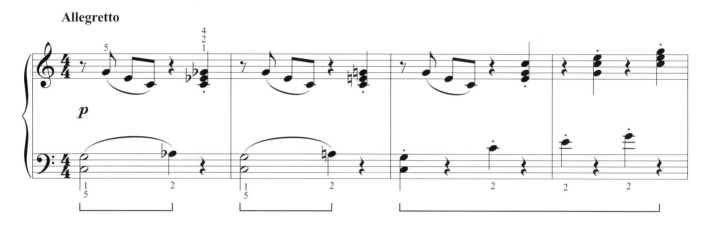

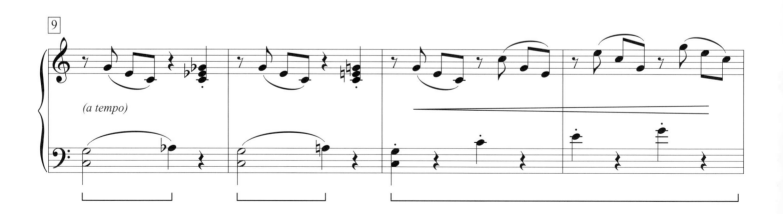

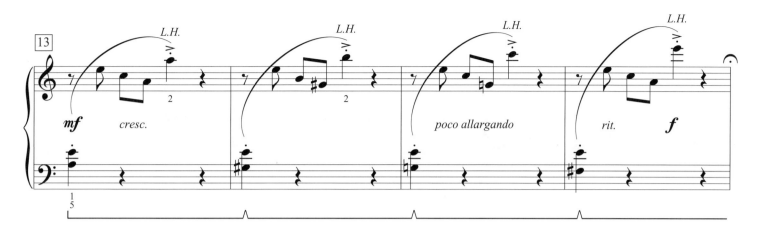

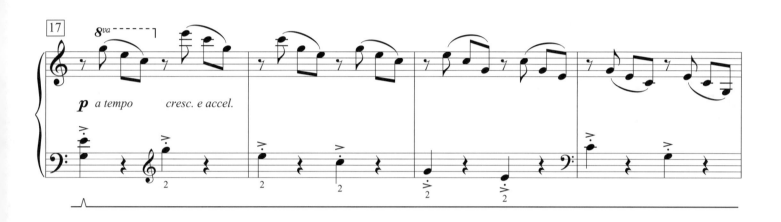

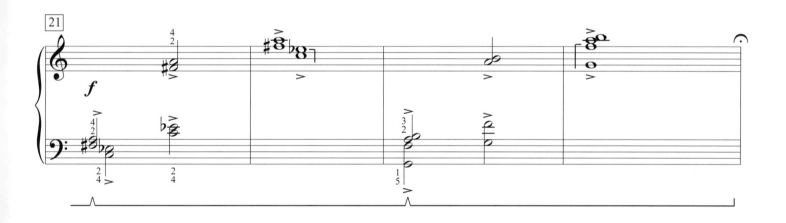

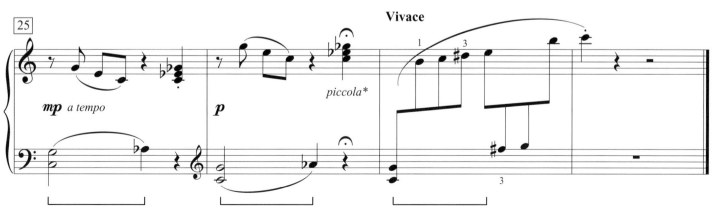

* Italian for "short"

Carnival in Rio

William Gillock

Tempo di Samba

NOTE: *Carnival in Rio* is also available as a piano duo (2 pianos, 4 hands).

To Donnagay Lynn

Dancing in a Dream

William Gillock

Allegretto; con rubato

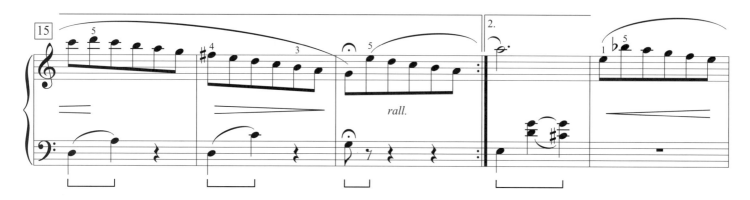

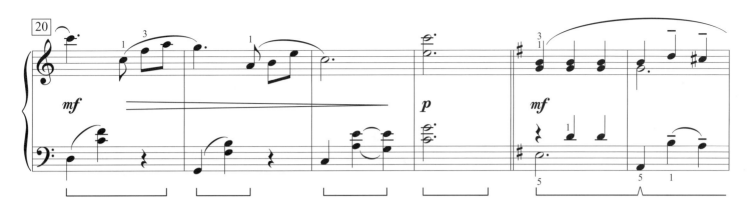

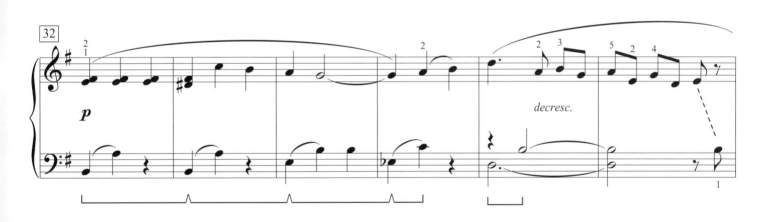

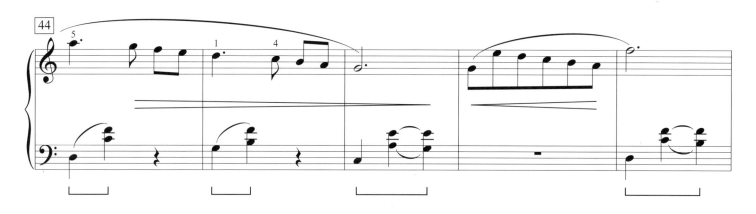

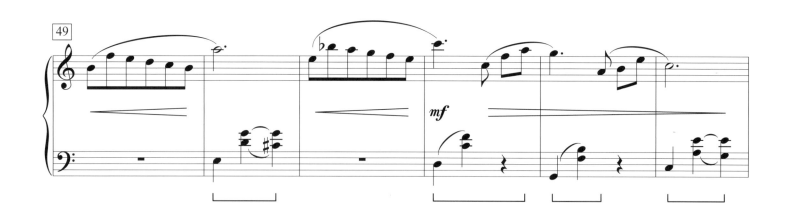

gradually return to *a tempo*

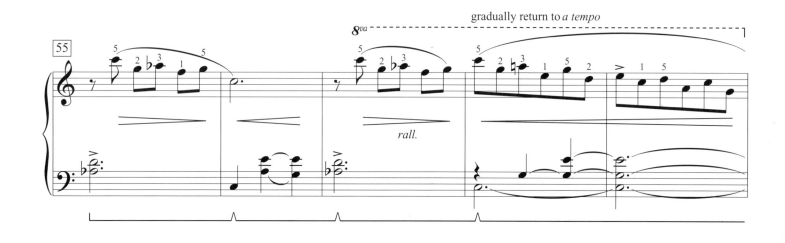

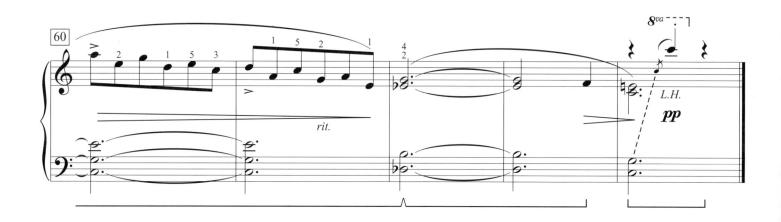

Fondly dedicated to the 80th anniversary of
The New Orleans Music Teachers Association

Deserted Plantation

William Gillock

Downtown Beat

William Gillock

Etude in A Major
(The Coral Sea)

William Gillock

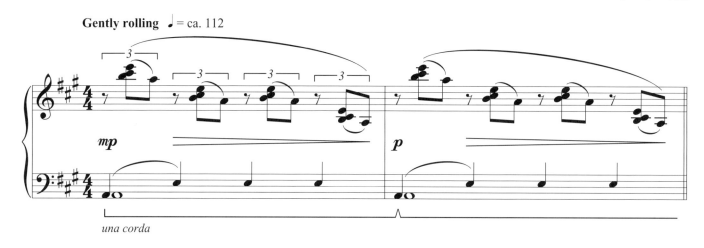

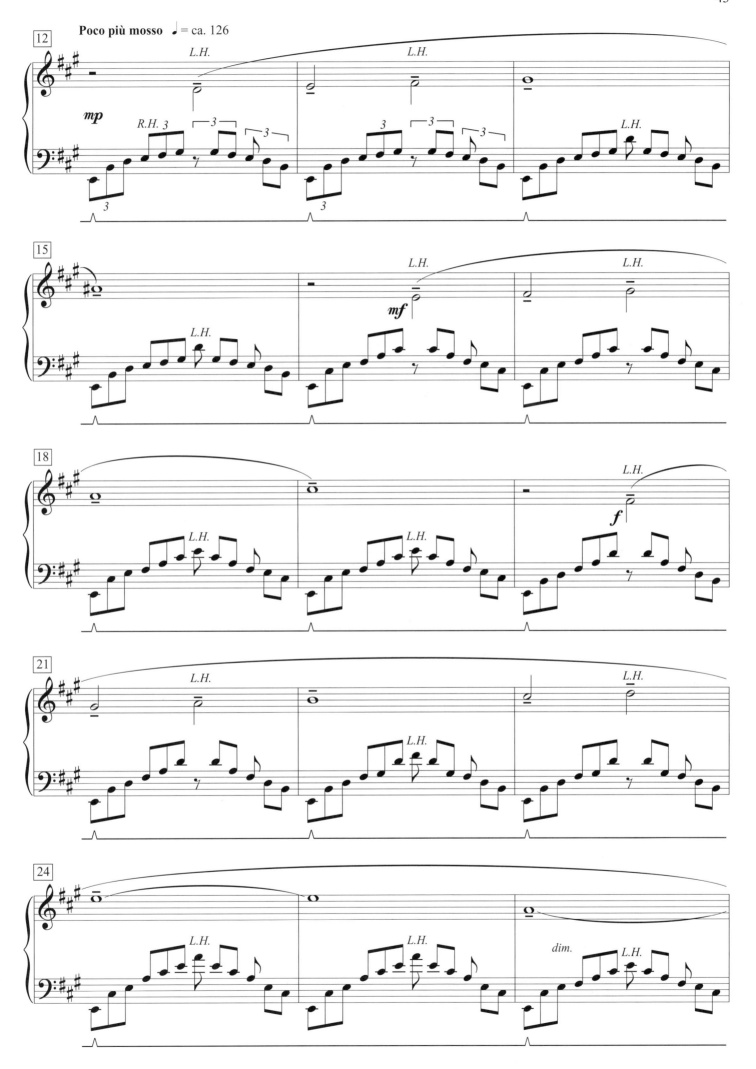

To the Lakeview Metronome Club of New Orleans

Fountain in the Rain

William Gillock

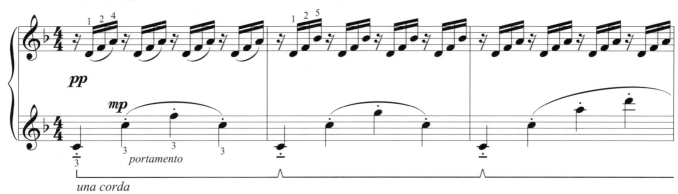

To Tommy Eaton

Festive Piece

William Gillock

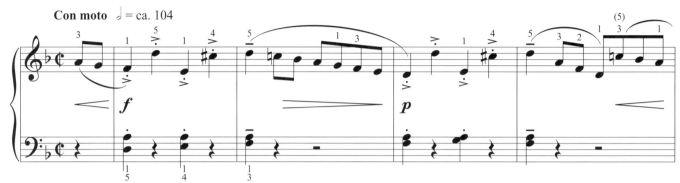

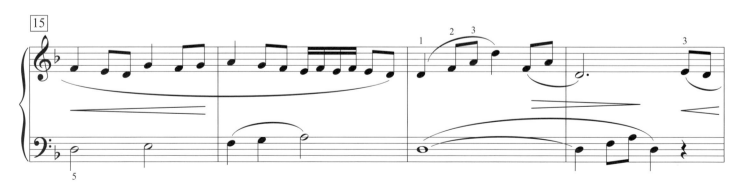

Flamenco

William Gillock

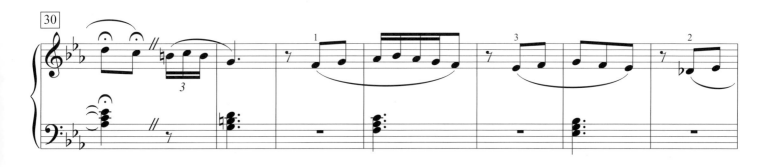

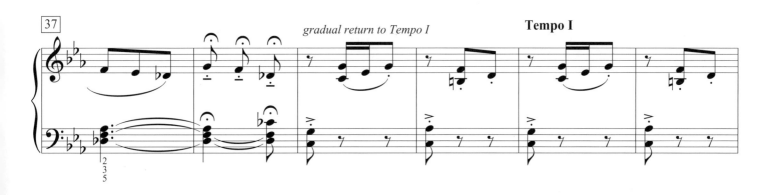

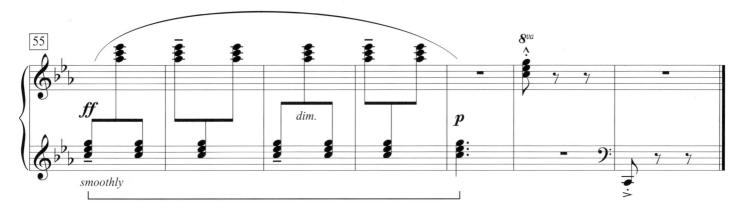

Happy Birthday to You

*For Richard Rejino, on the occasion of his 30th birthday
at the National Piano Teachers Institute, 1987*

Words and Music by Mildred J. Hill and Patty S. Hill
Arranged by William Gillock

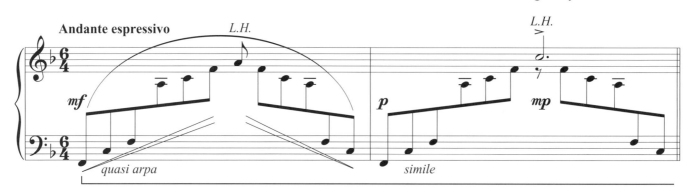

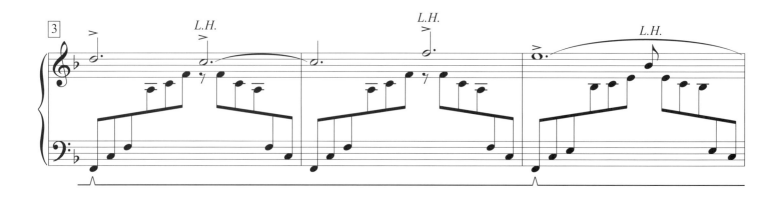

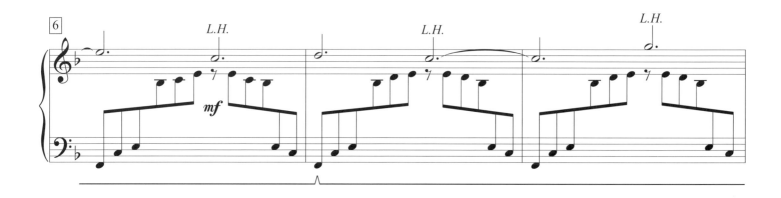

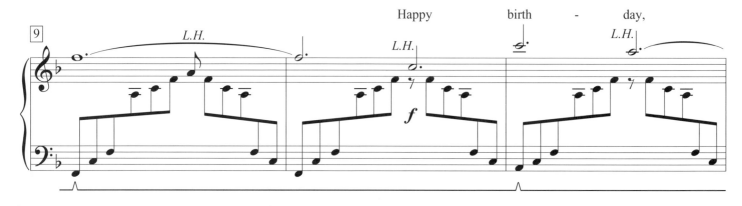

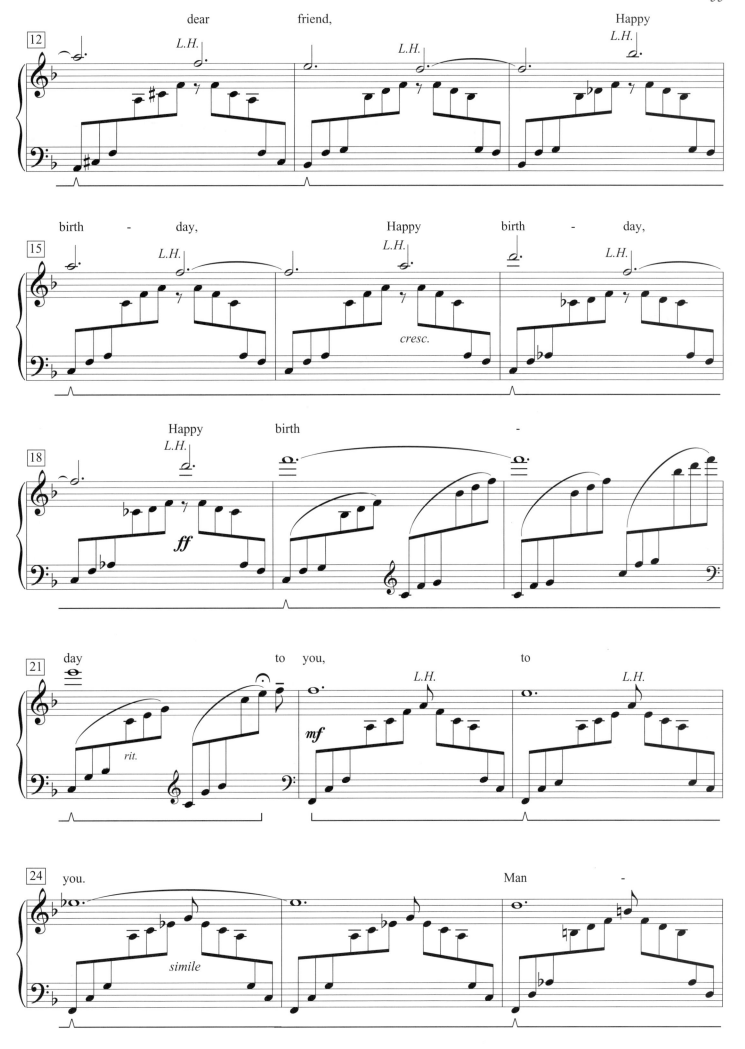

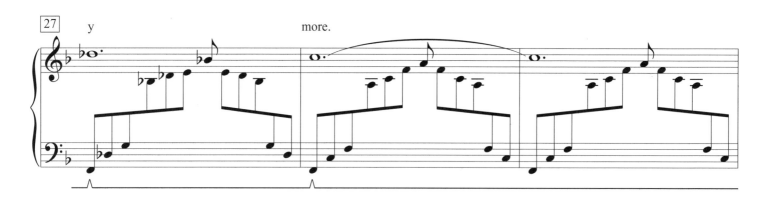

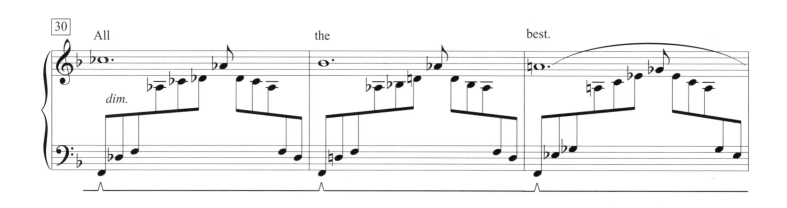

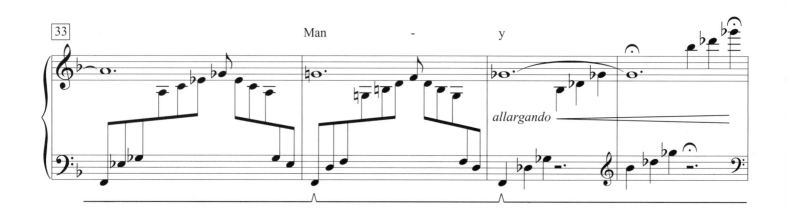

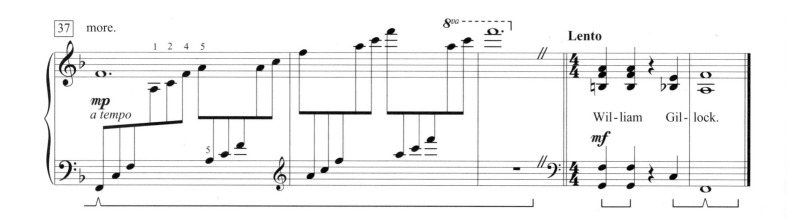

To the New Jersey Music Education Council, Inc.

Goldfish

William Gillock

In a flowing manner, but with much flexibility

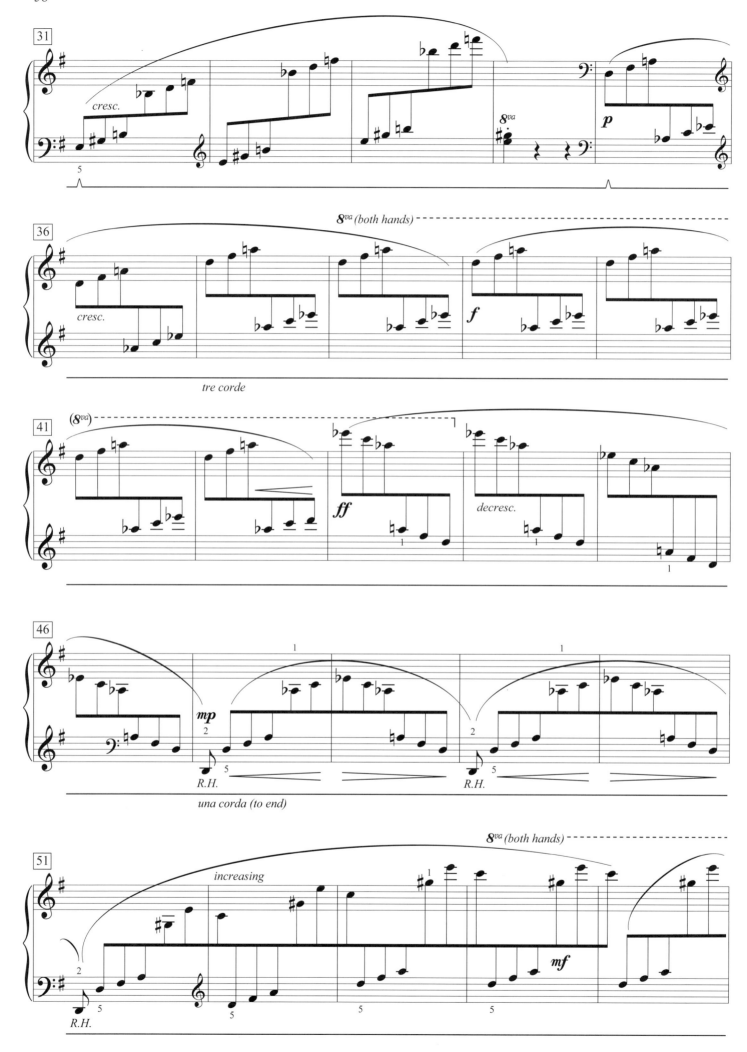

For Catherine Rollin

Homage to Chopin*

William Gillock

* First published as "Hommage to Chopin" in the key of G-sharp Minor.

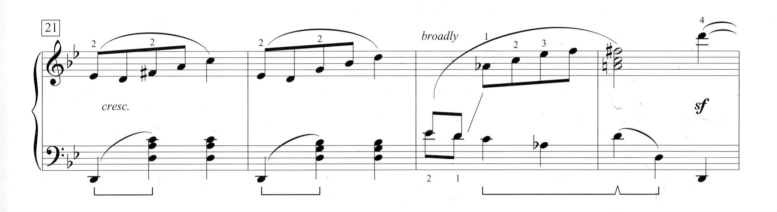

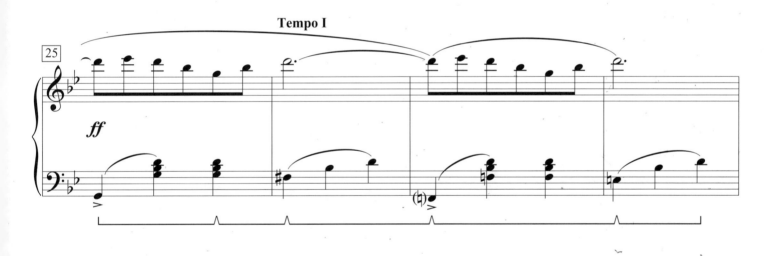

In Old Vienna

William Gillock

Tempo di valse Viennese

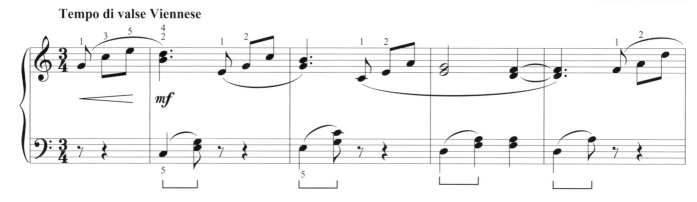

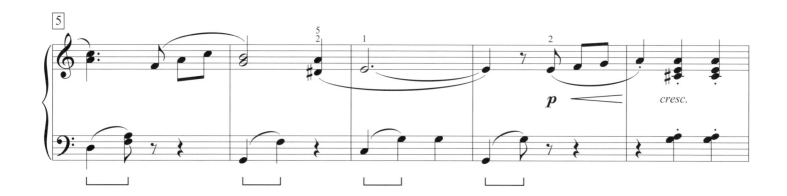

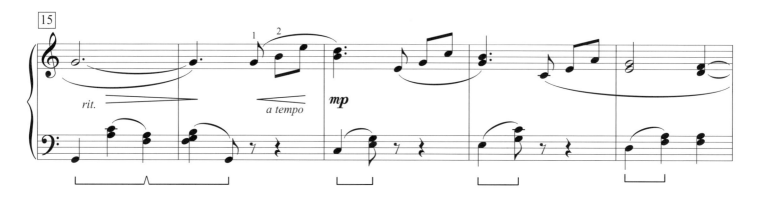

To Virginia Lum

Jazz Prelude

William Gillock

Fast; with rhythmic drive

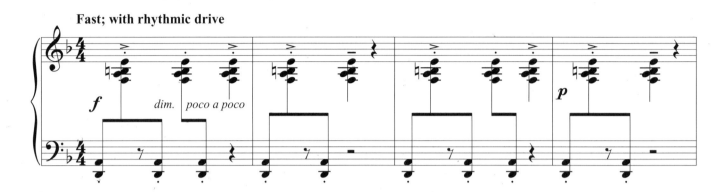

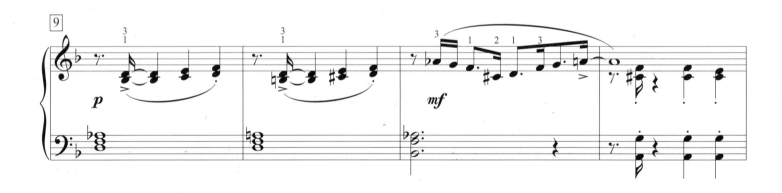

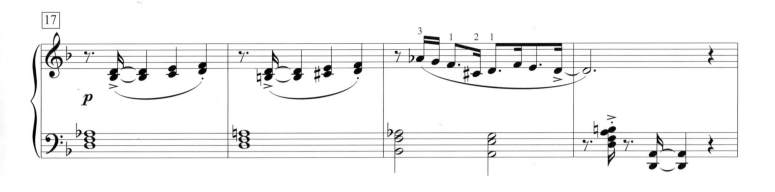

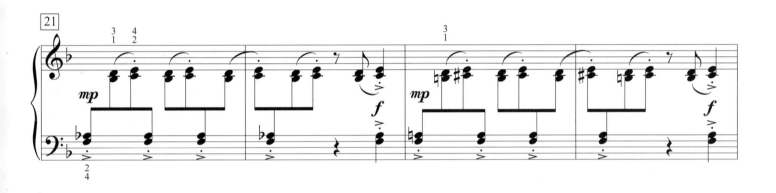

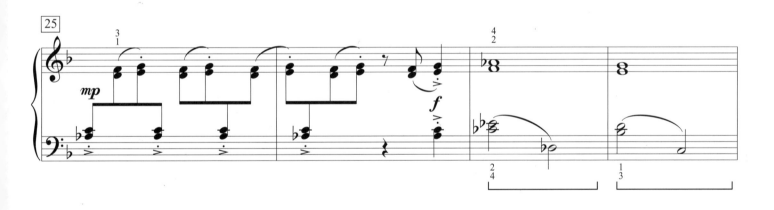

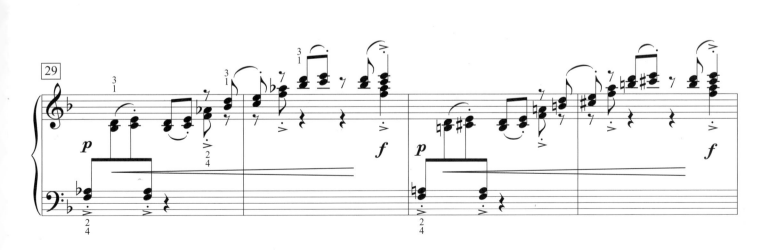

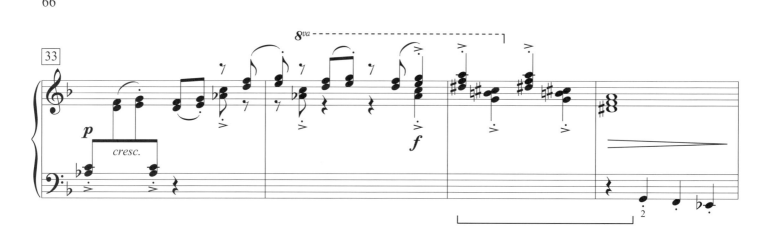

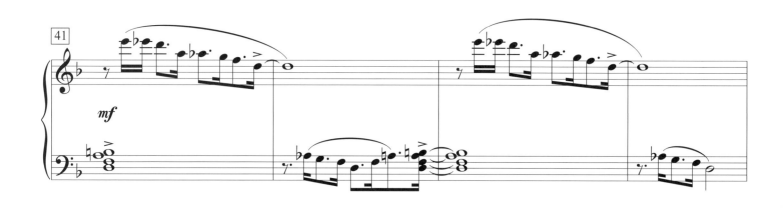

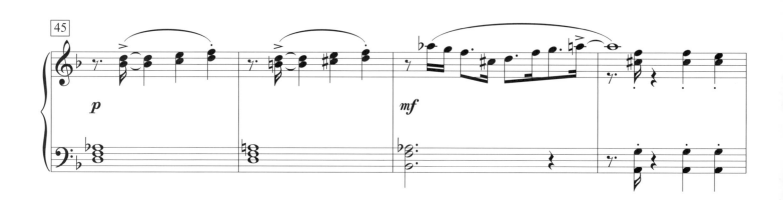

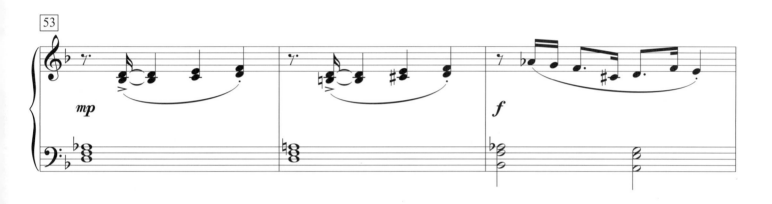

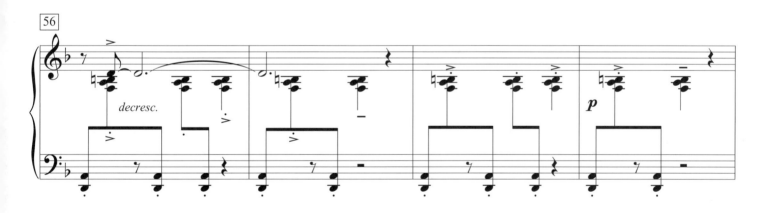

Journey in the Night

William Gillock

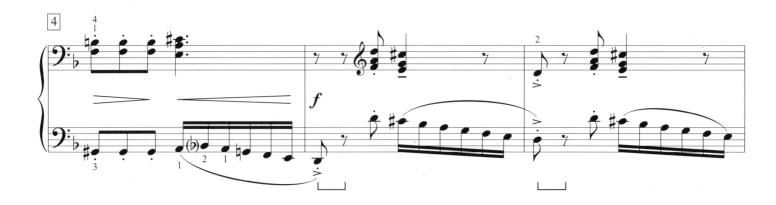

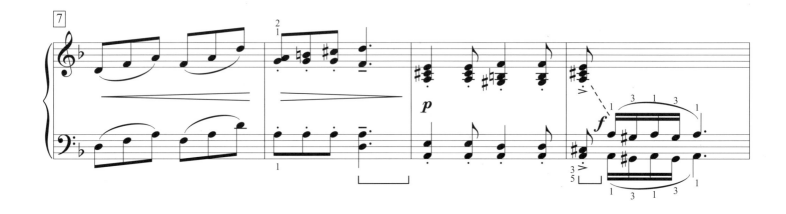

To Ruth Baskett

Lazy Bayou

William Gillock

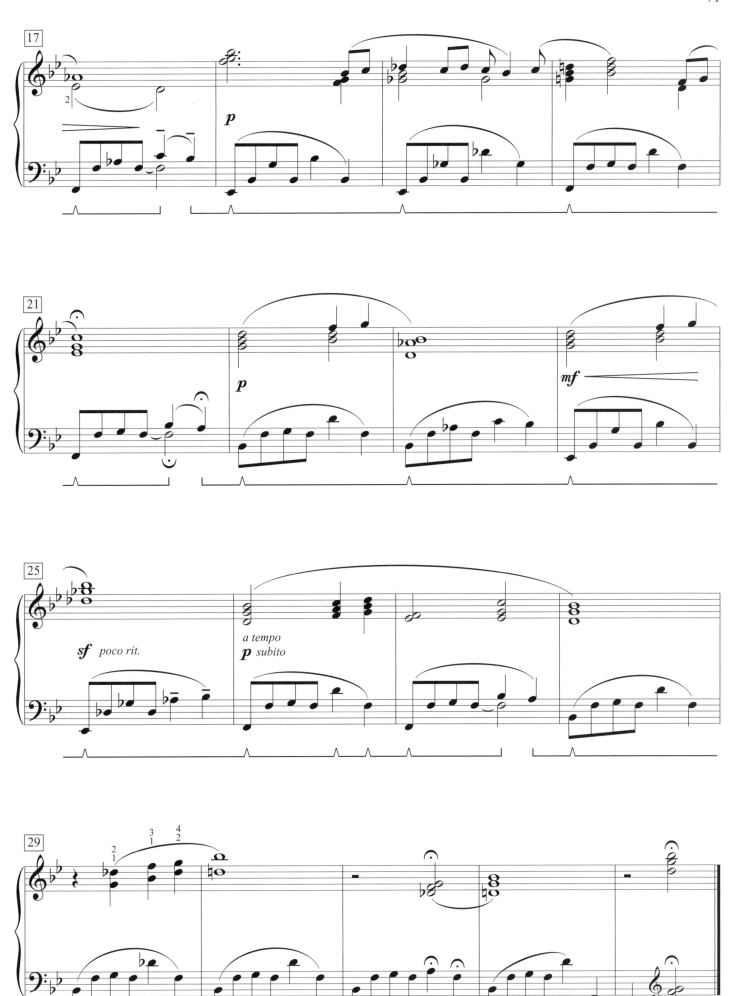

For Charlotte M. L. Willis

Little Suite in Baroque Style

I. Prelude

William Gillock

II. Festive March

III. Song of the Troubador

IV. Lively Dance

Mardi Gras

William Gillock

To Eugenia O'Reilly

A Memory of Vienna

William Gillock

Tempo di valse lento, con molto rubato

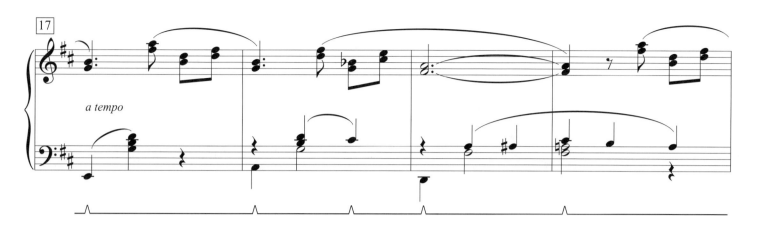

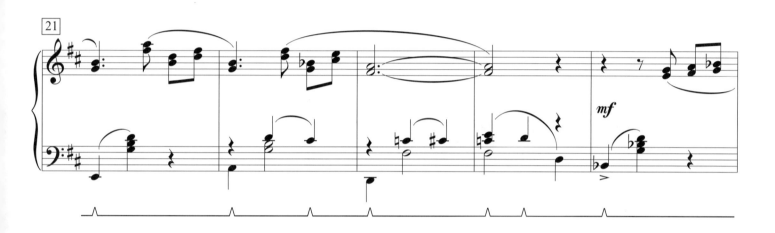

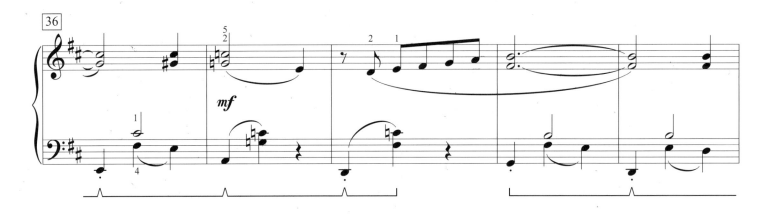

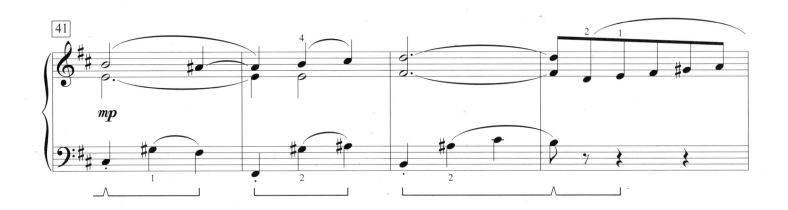

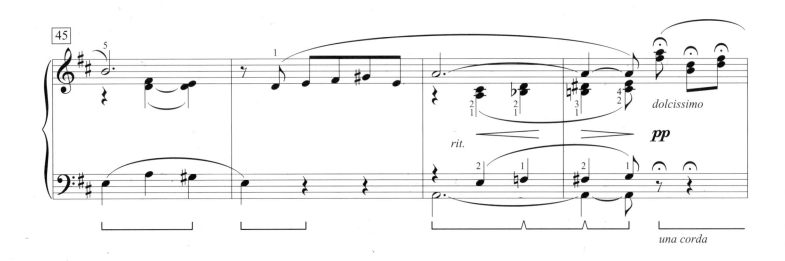

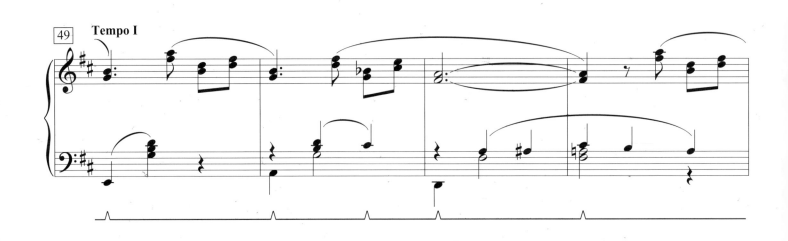

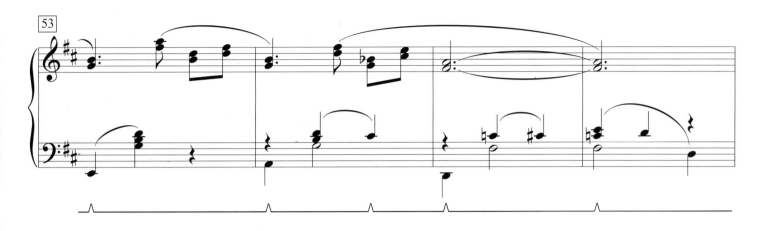

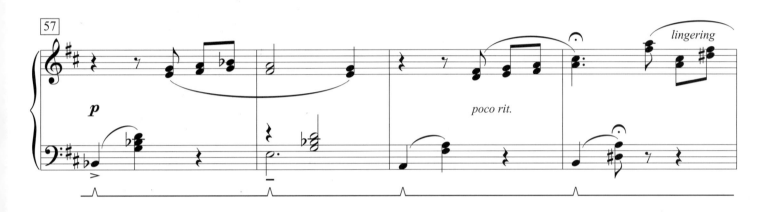

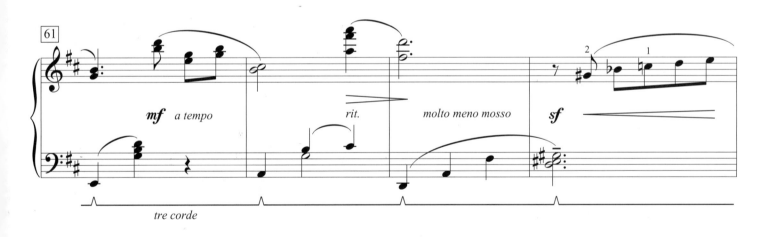

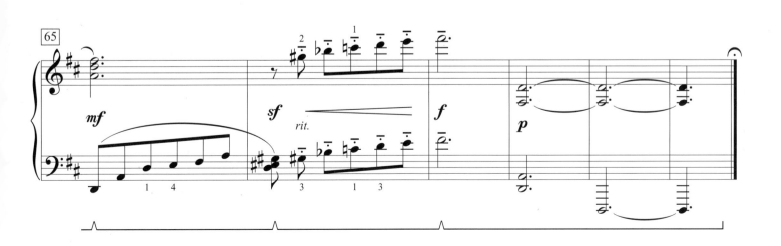

New Orleans Nightfall

William Gillock

Tempo I, but with a more pronounced beat

For the 25th Anniversary of the Joplin, Missouri Piano Teachers' Association

Night Serenade

William Gillock

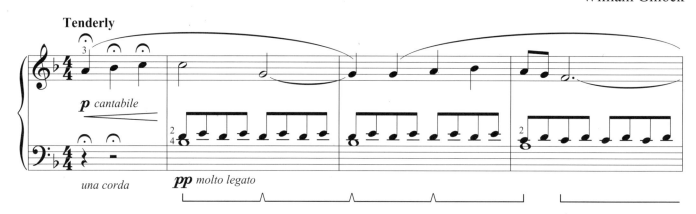

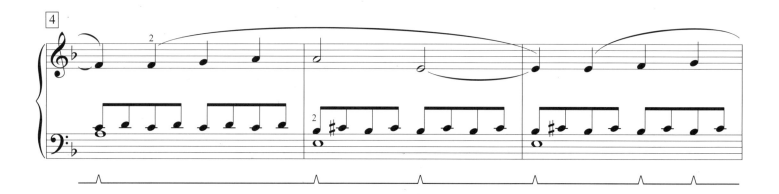

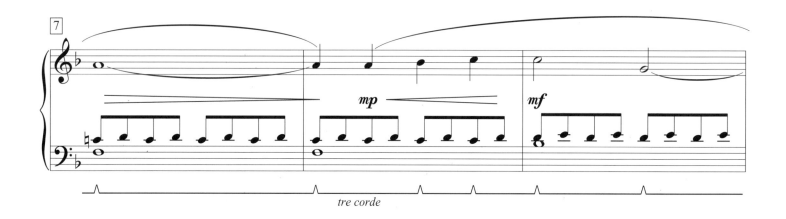

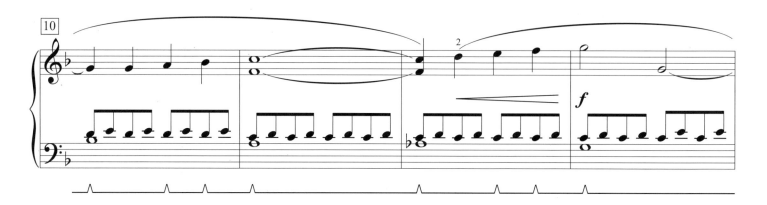

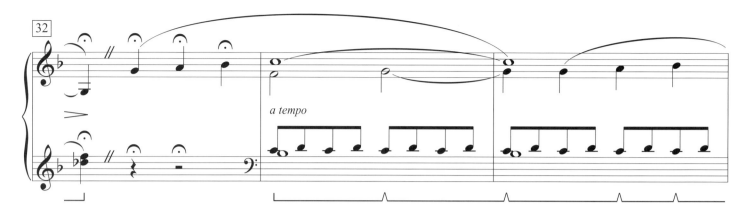

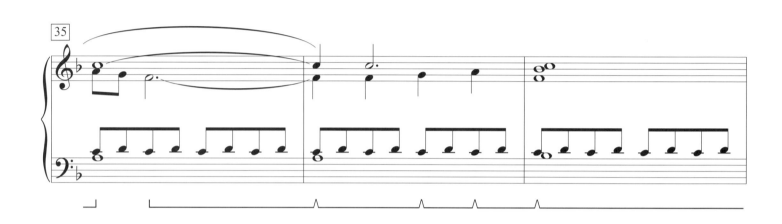

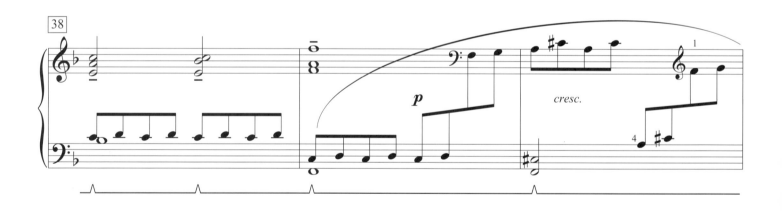

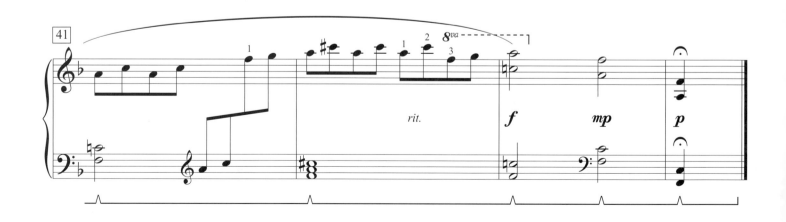

To Ruth Adele Miller

On a Paris Boulevard

William Gillock

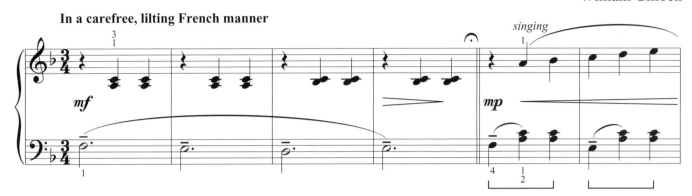

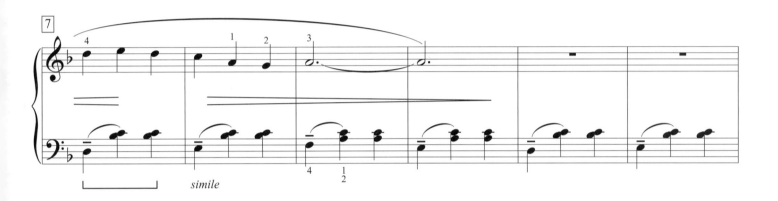

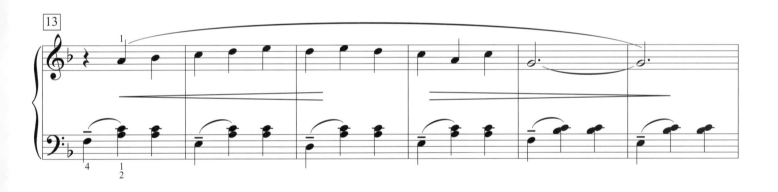

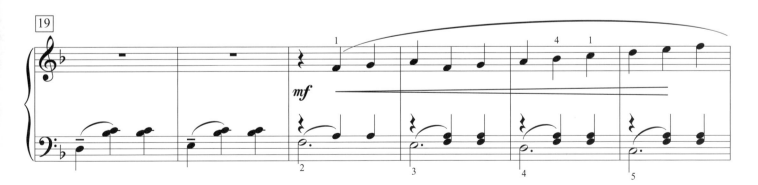

NOTE: *On a Paris Boulevard* is also available as a piano duo (2 pianos, 4 hands).

To Robert Harris

Nocturne

William Gillock

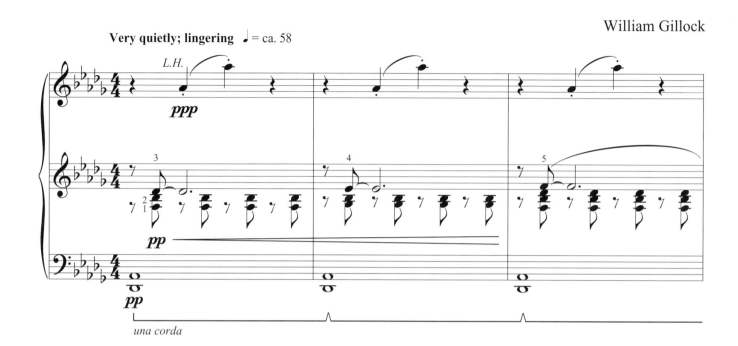

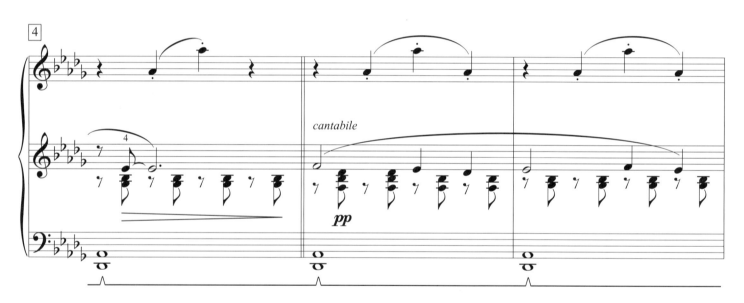

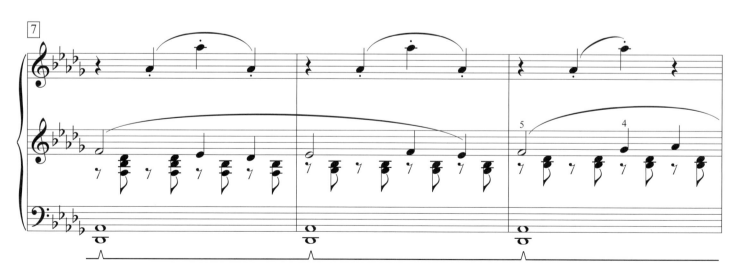

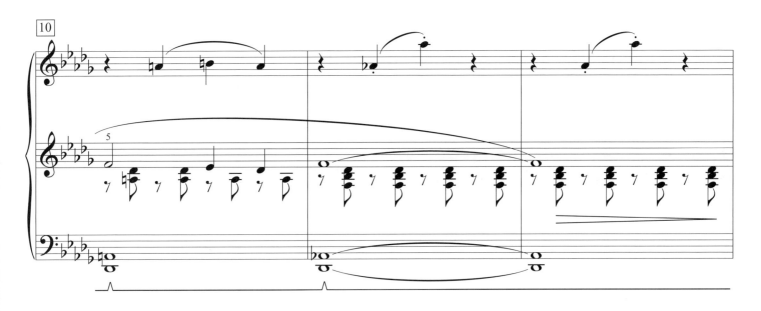

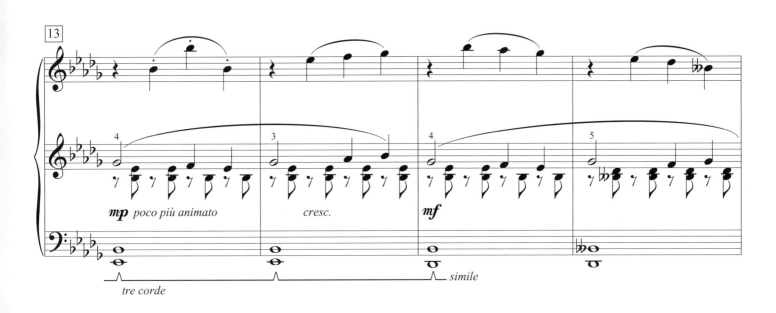

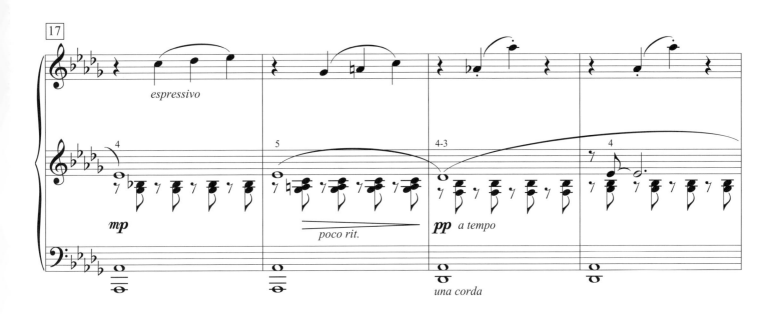

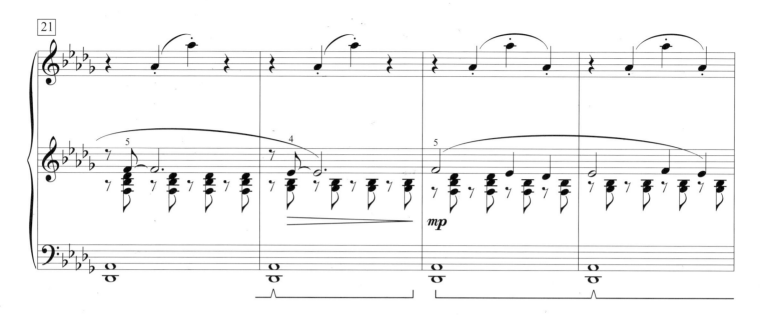

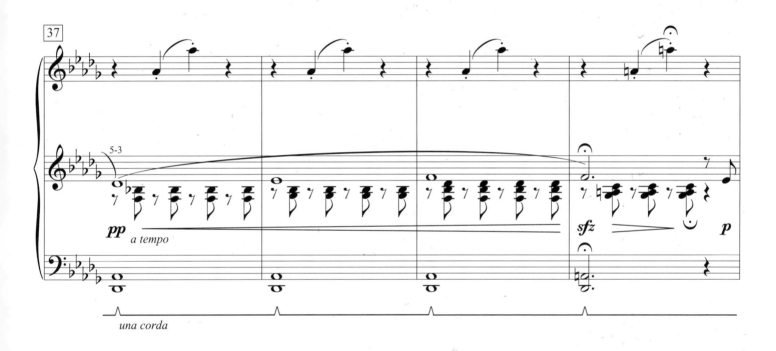

For Glenda Austin

On the Champs-Élysées

William Gillock

With a steady dance beat and minimal rhythmic nuance

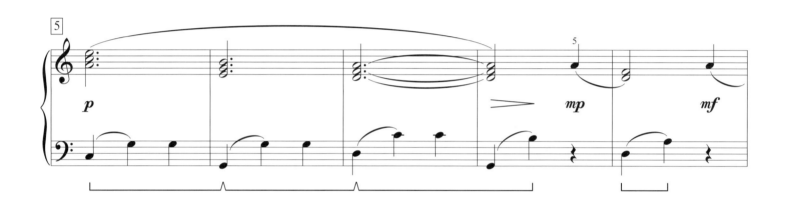

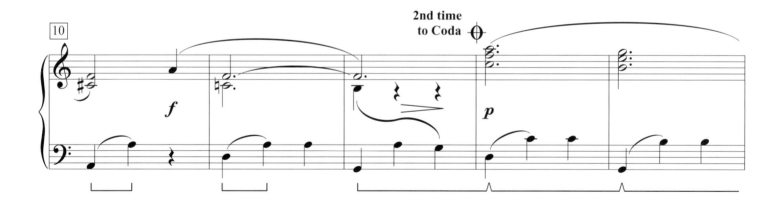

* Original key D-flat Major.

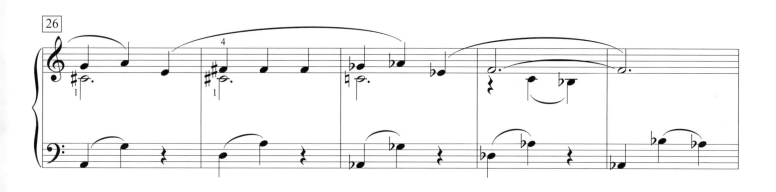

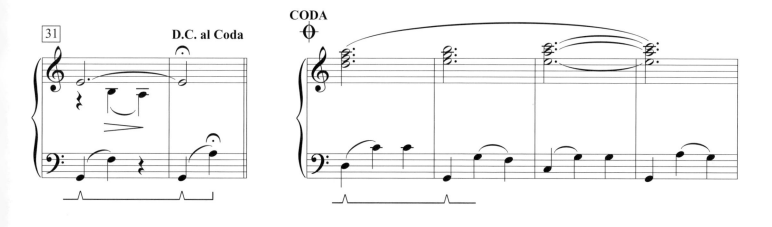

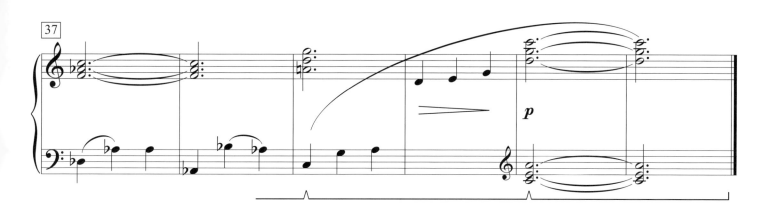

For Enid Wheeler

Petite Etude

William Gillock

To the Hawai'i chapter of the National Guild of Piano Teachers

Polynesian Nocturne

William Gillock

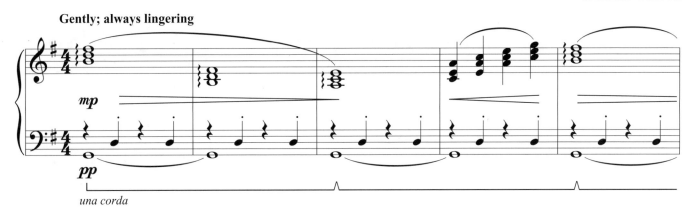

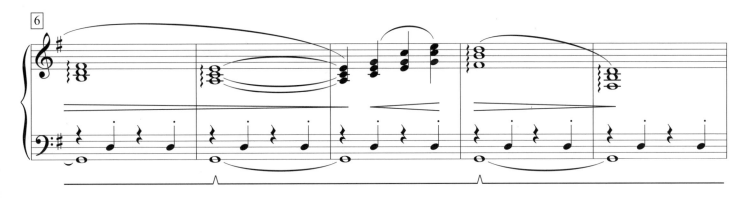

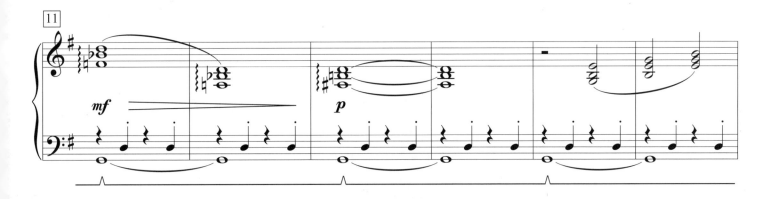

To Earl Jones
Portrait of Paris

William Gillock

Vivaciously, but with romantic tempo liberties

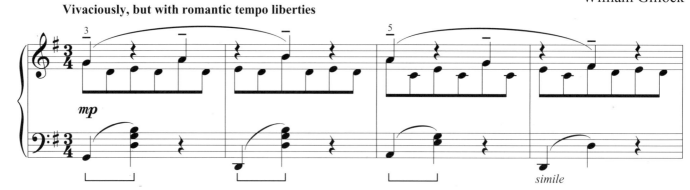

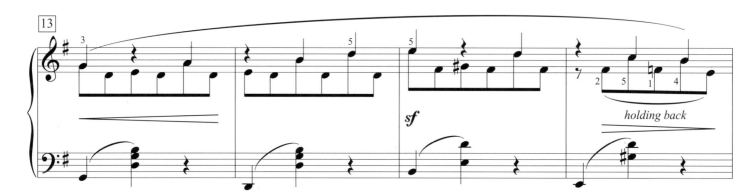

NOTE: *Portrait of Paris* is also available as a piano duo (2 pianos, 4 hands).

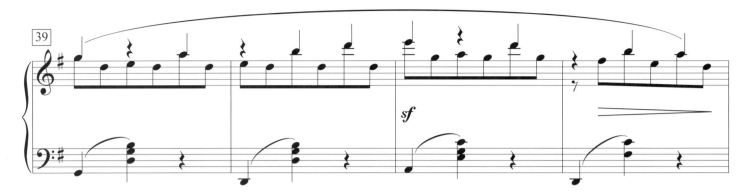

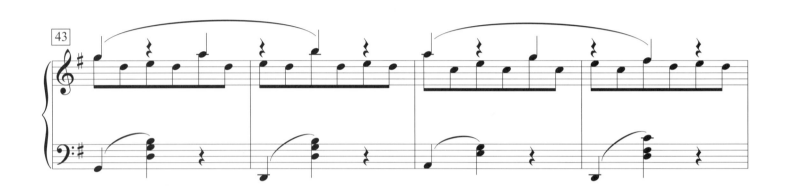

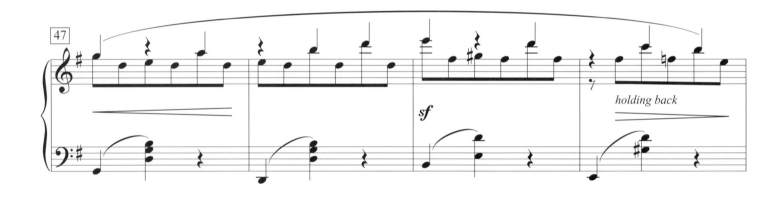

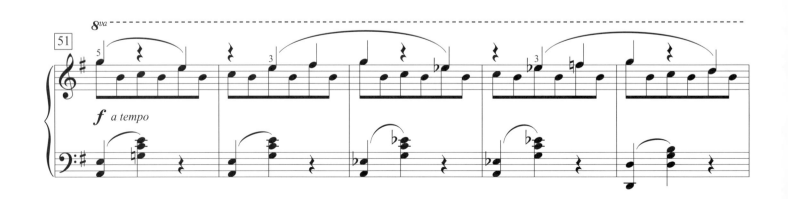

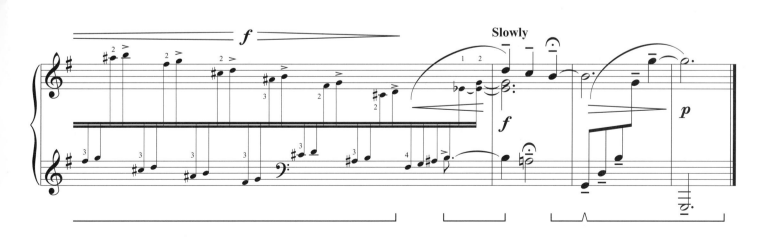

To Mildred R. Dalton

Sarabande

William Gillock

Slowly, with grace ♩ = 54–58

* Accompaniment *portato* throughout.

To Marvin Kahn

Sleighbells in the Snow

William Gillock

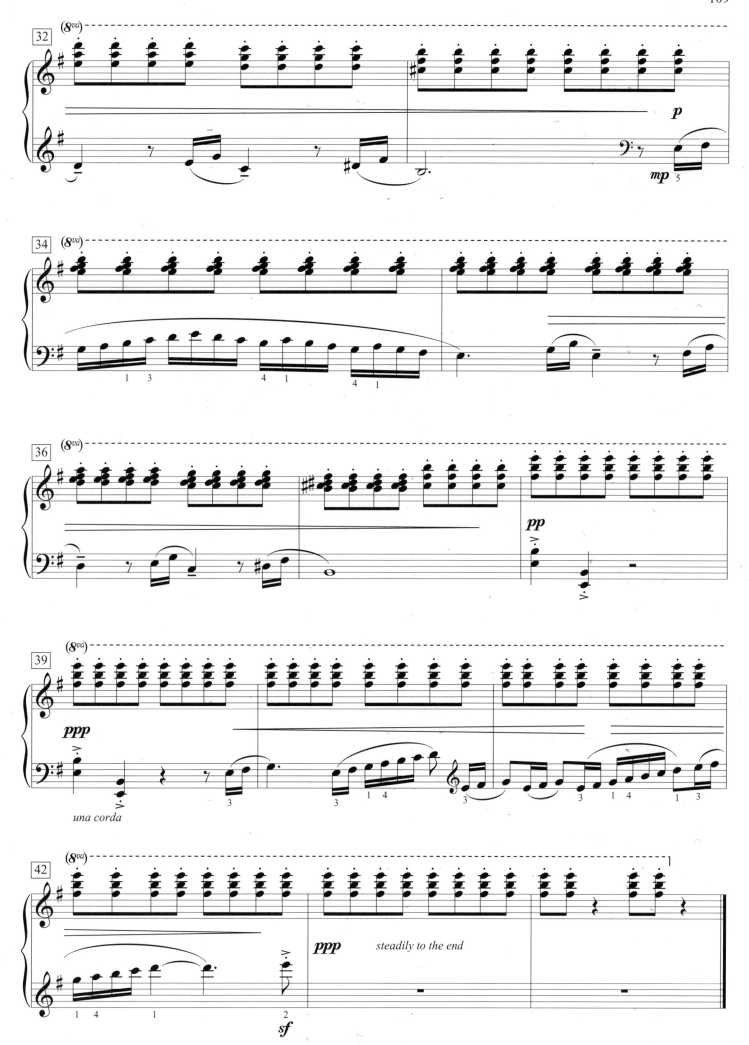

To Everett Stevens

Sleigh Ride

William Gillock

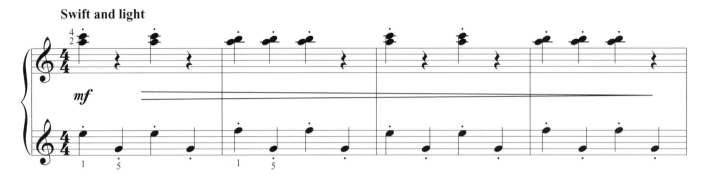

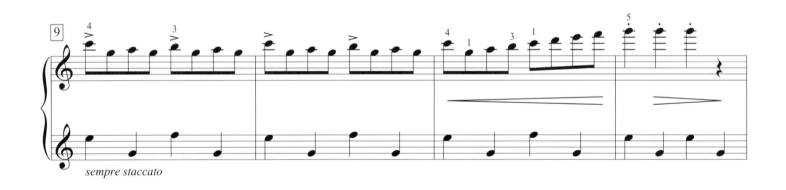

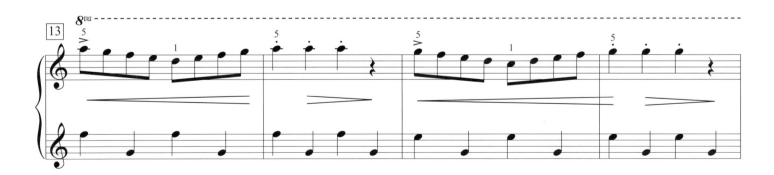

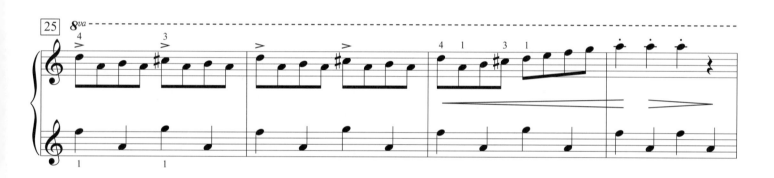

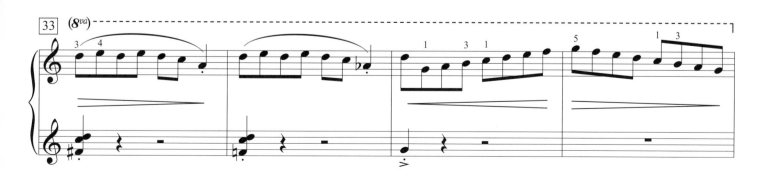

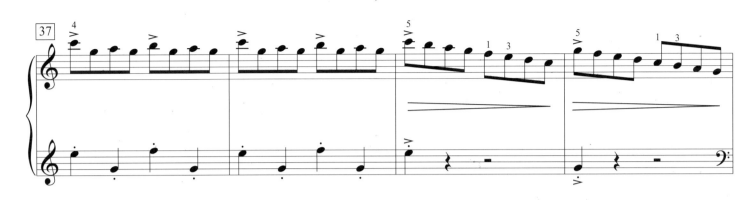

growing more and more distant

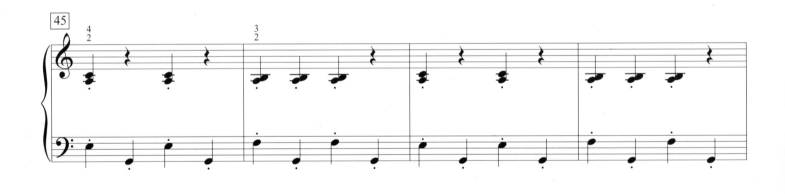

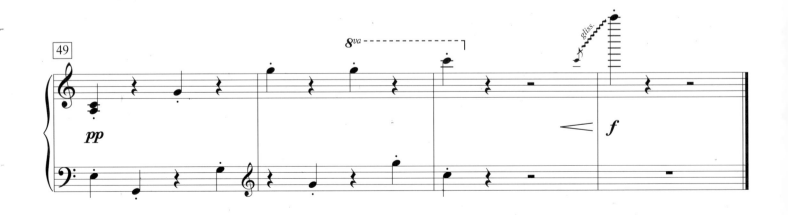

For Susan Alexander

Slumber Song

William Gillock

© 1969 by The Willis Music Co.
Copyright Renewed
International Copyright Secured   All Rights Reserved

To George Kelver

Sonatine

William Gillock

I. Moderately fast ♩ = ca. 132

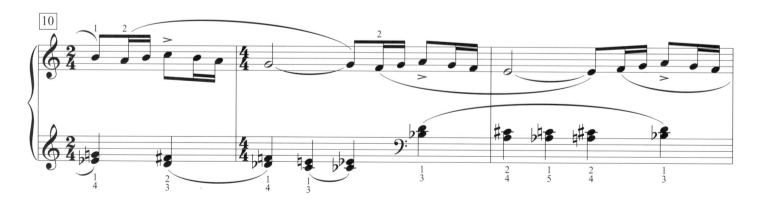

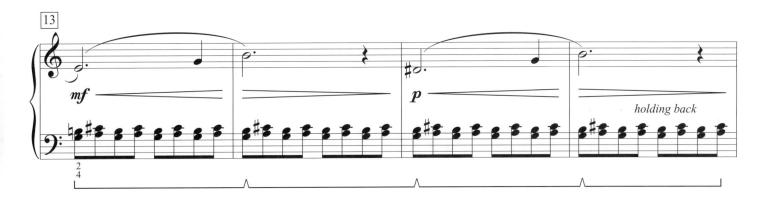

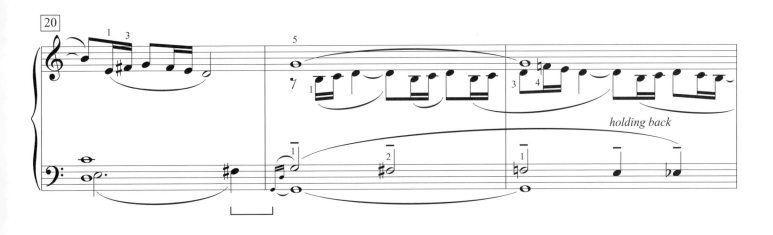

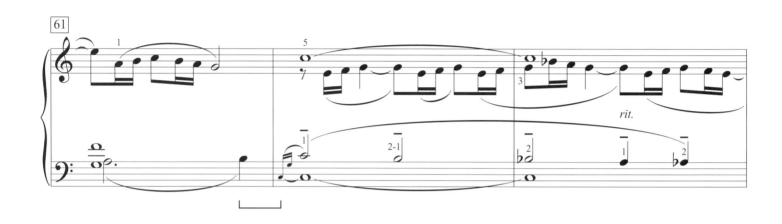

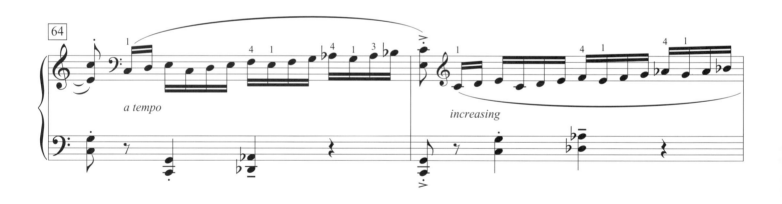

II. Slowly, with drowsy movement ♪ = ca. 116

una corda

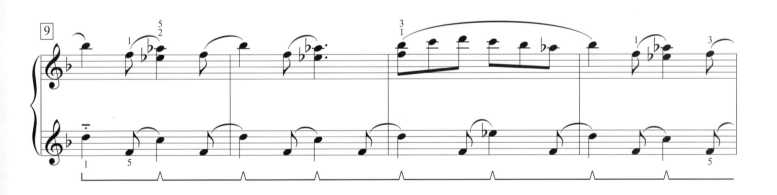

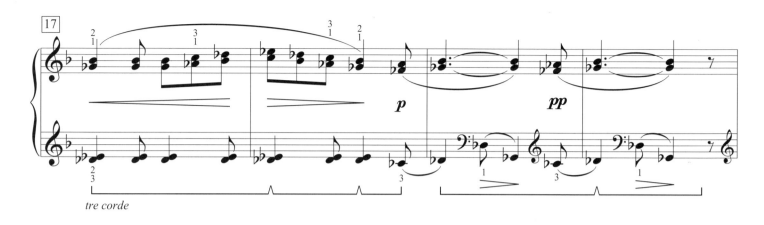

tre corde

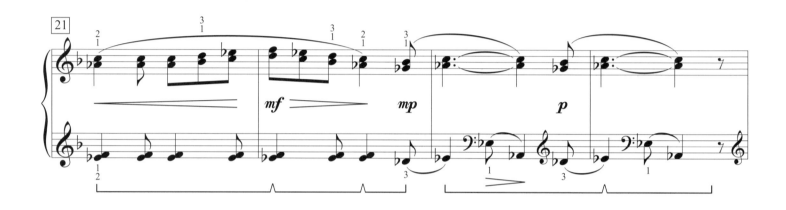

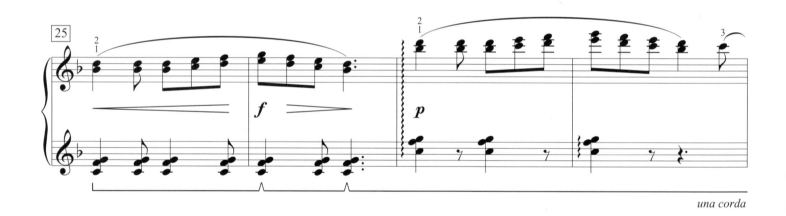

una corda

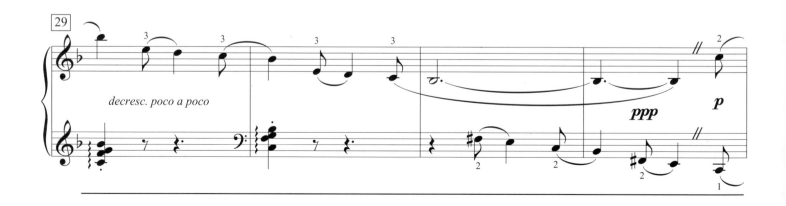

decresc. poco a poco

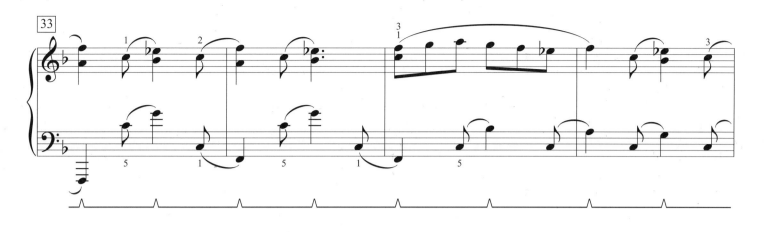

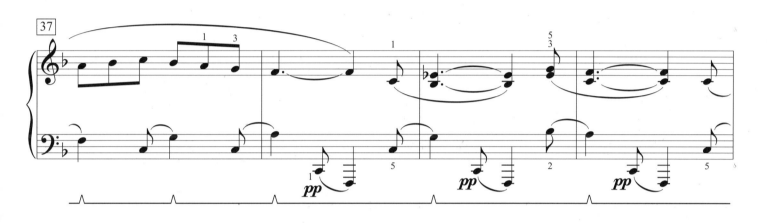

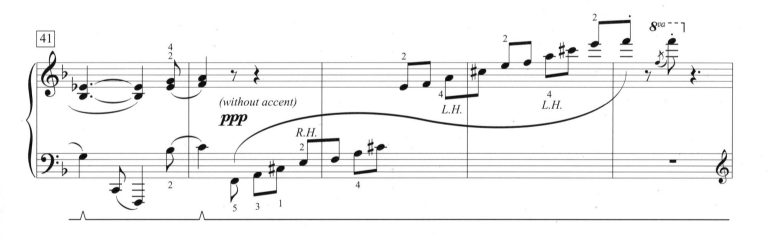

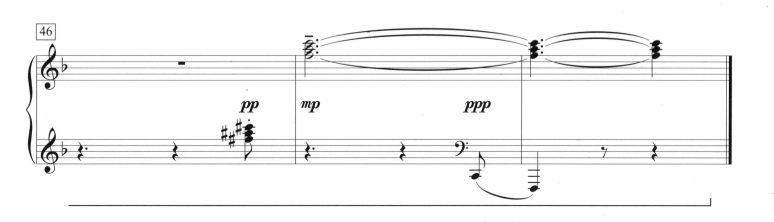

III. Rondo; vigorously, rhythmically ($\quarternote$ = ca. 138)

To the students of Carolyn Jones Campbell

Sonatina in G

William Gillock

I. Allegro moderato

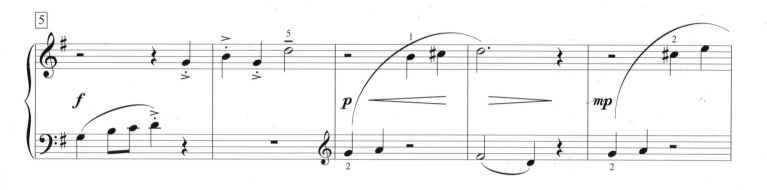

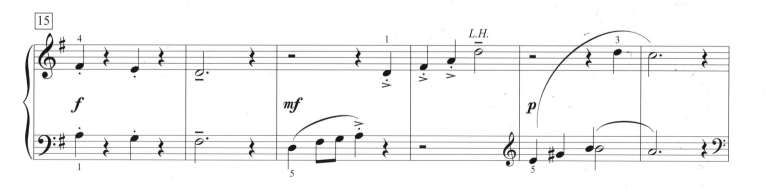

II. Valse sentimentale

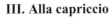

III. Alla capriccio

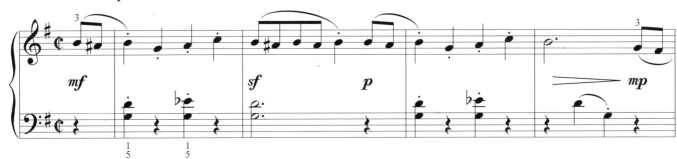

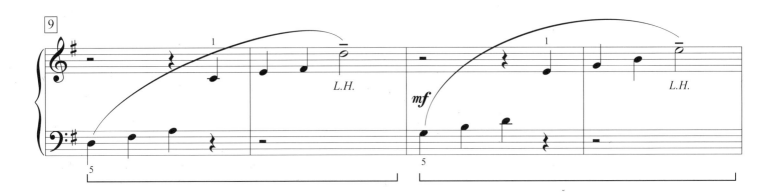

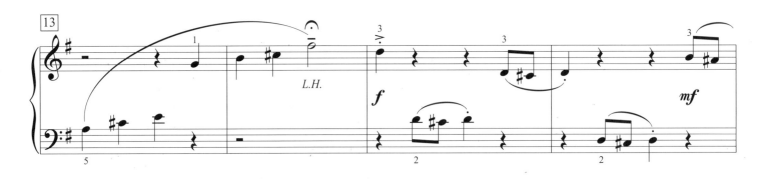

Spanish Gypsies

William Gillock

Flamenco style; intensely rhythmic

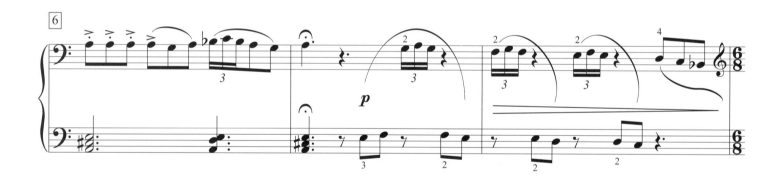

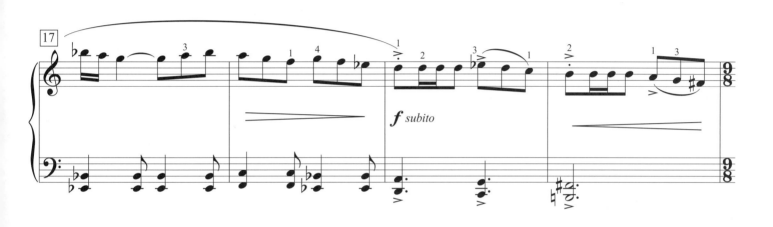

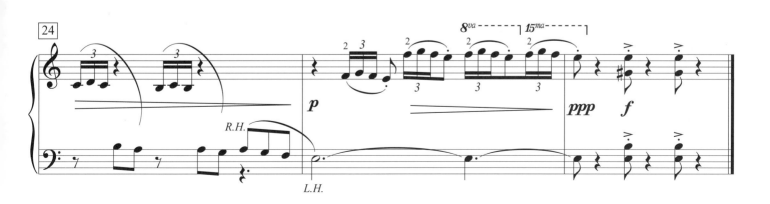

Star Dancers

William Gillock

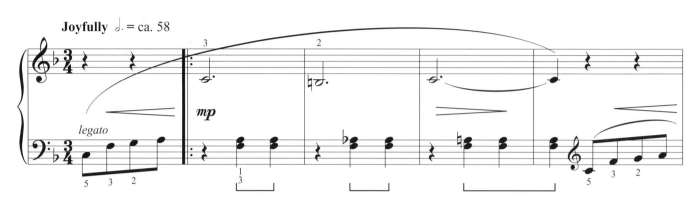

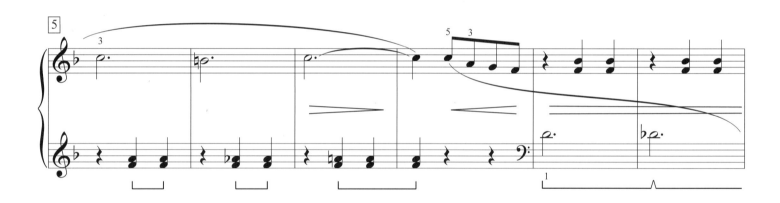

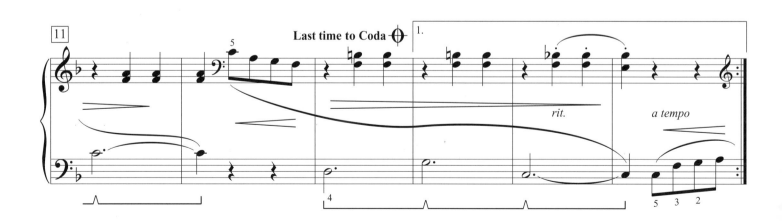

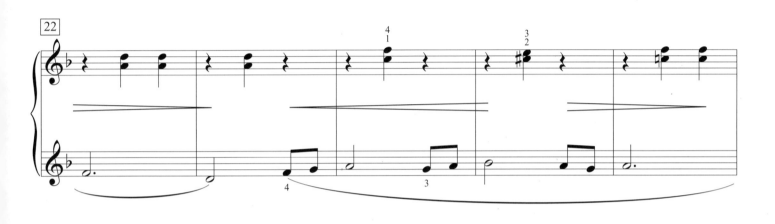

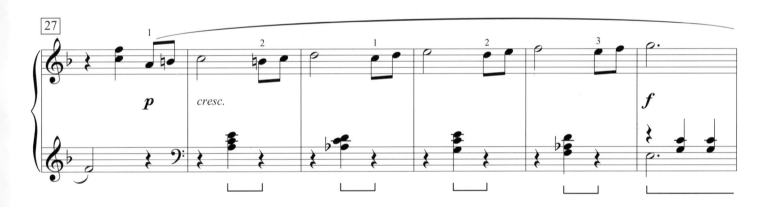

D.C. al Coda
(with repeat)

CODA

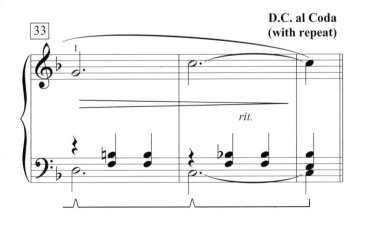

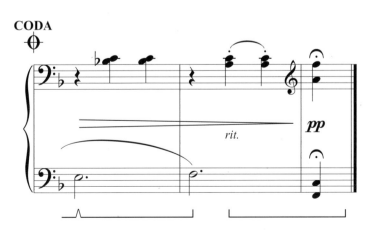

Sunset

William Gillock

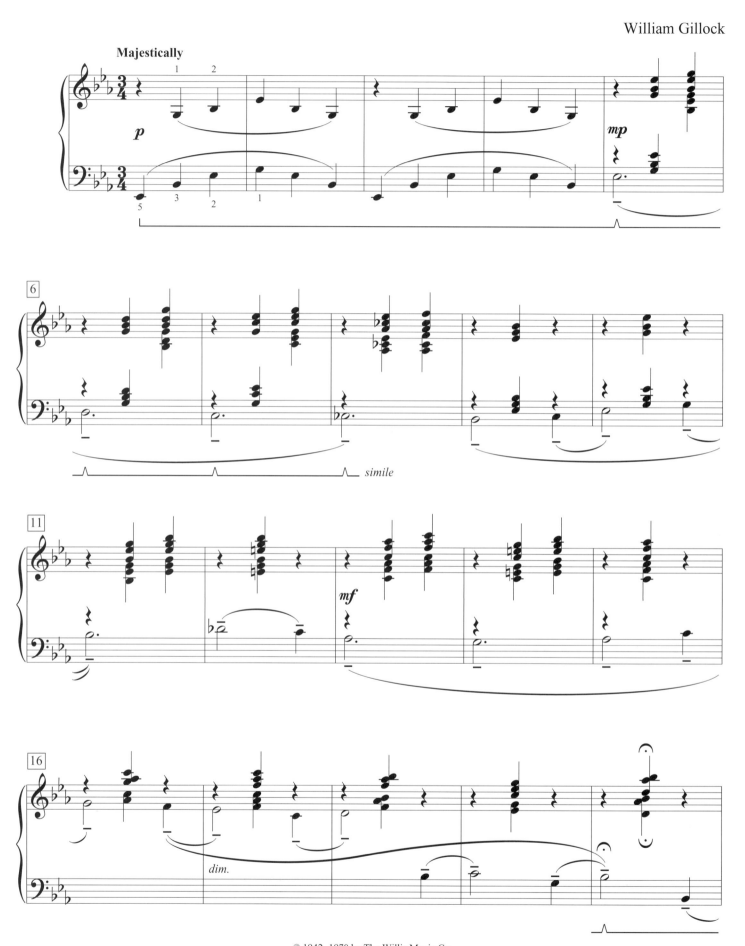

* Both hands *8va* on half notes.

Tarantella

William Gillock

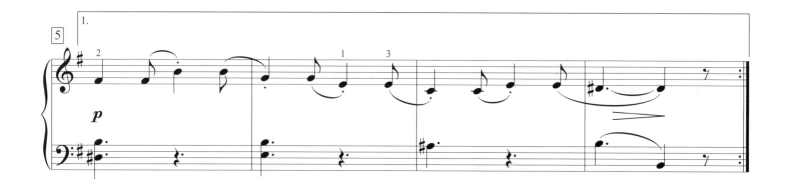

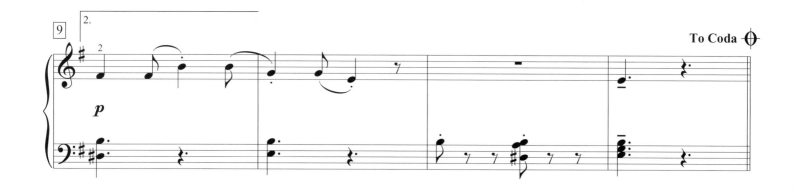

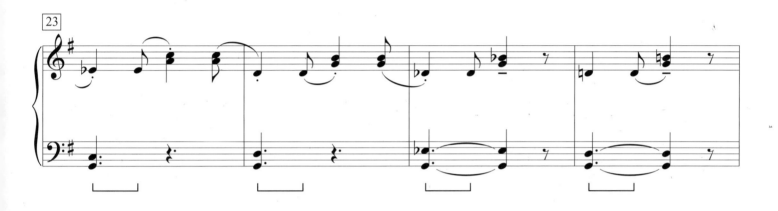

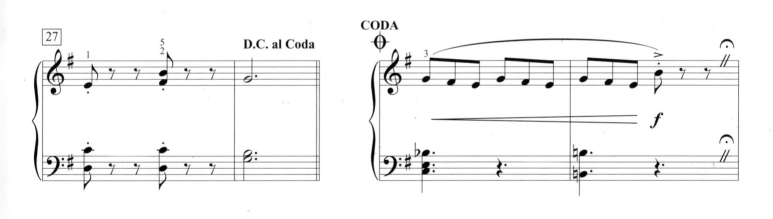

Third Sonatina
(Sonatina in C)

William Gillock

I. Allegretto grazioso

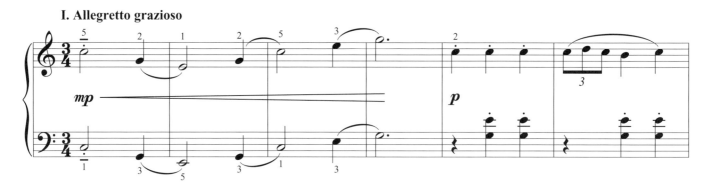

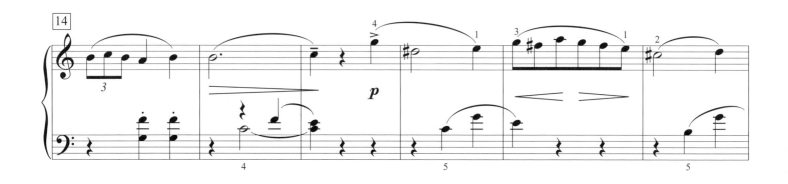

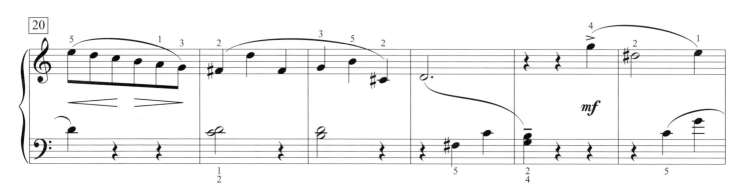

II. Tempo di menuetto

cantabile

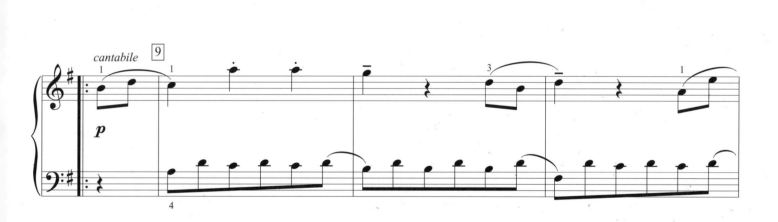

Last time to Coda

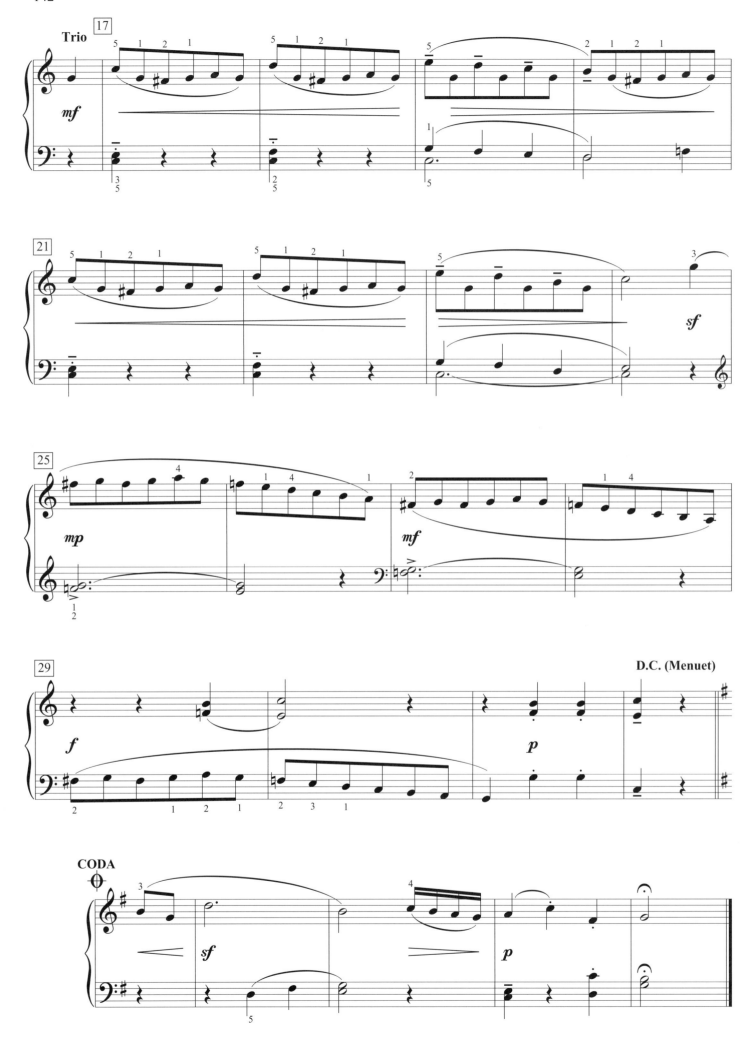

III. Spiritoso vivace

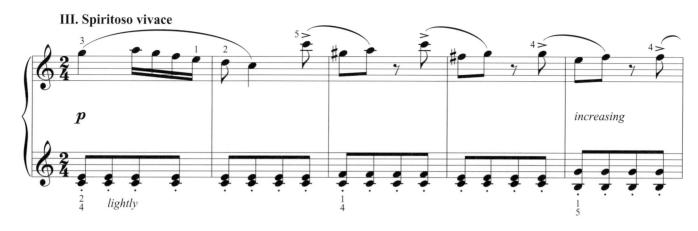

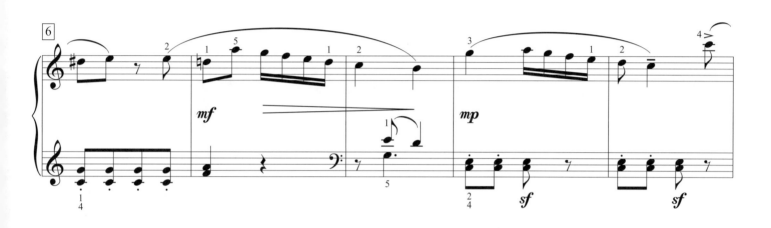

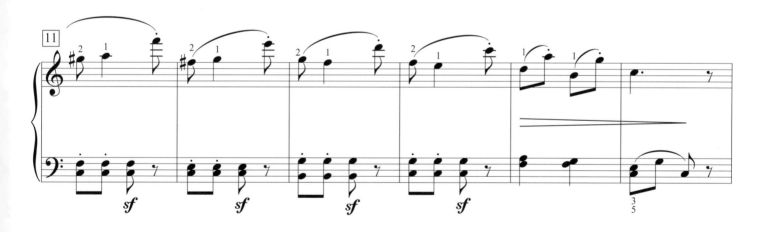

Uptown Blues

William Gillock

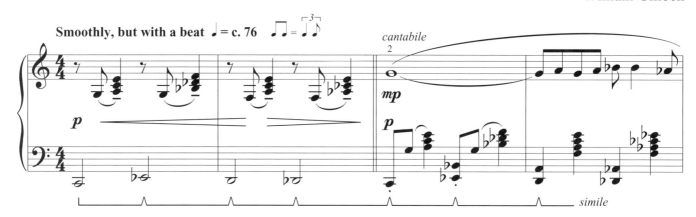

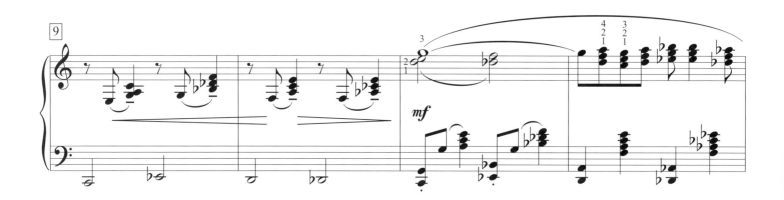

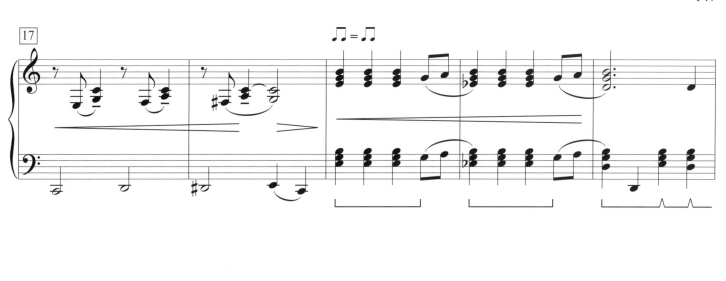

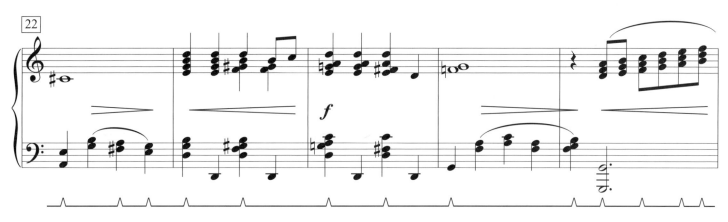

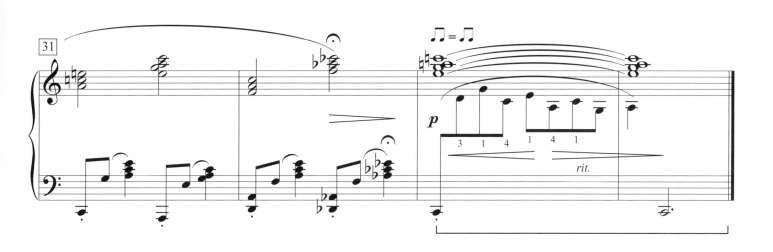

Valse Etude

Especially for Student Affiliate of Dallas Music Teachers' Association

William Gillock

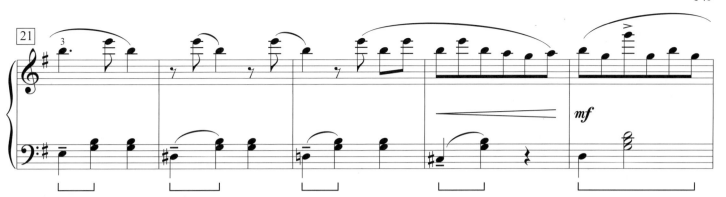

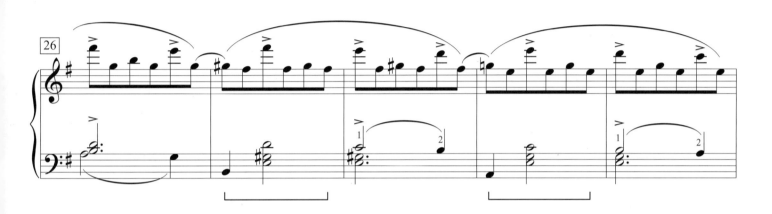

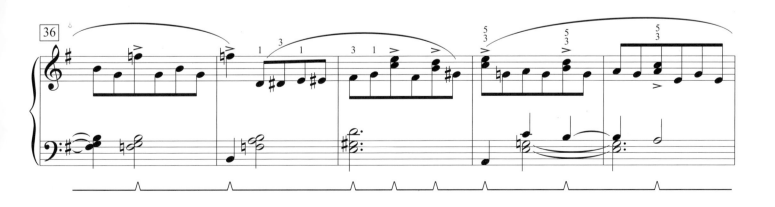

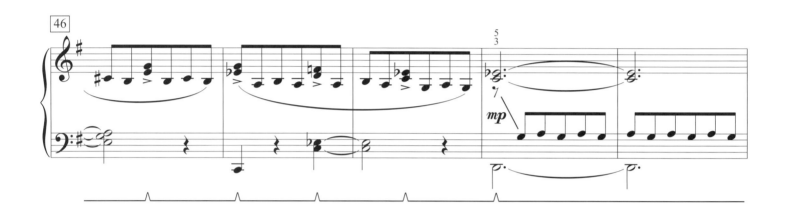

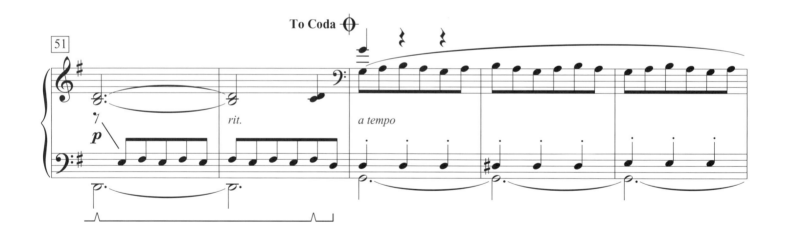

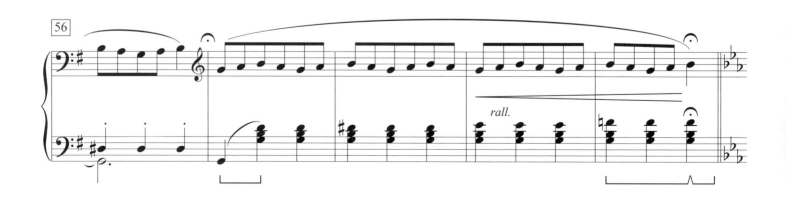

Meno mosso e molto lirico

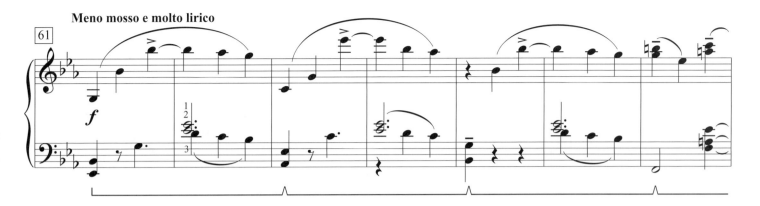

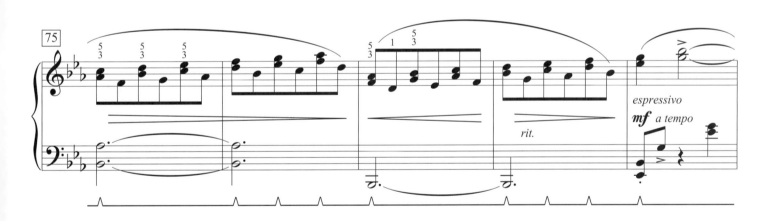

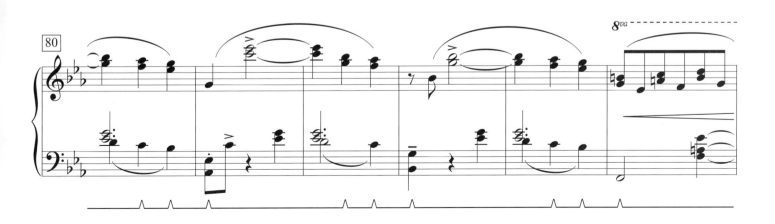

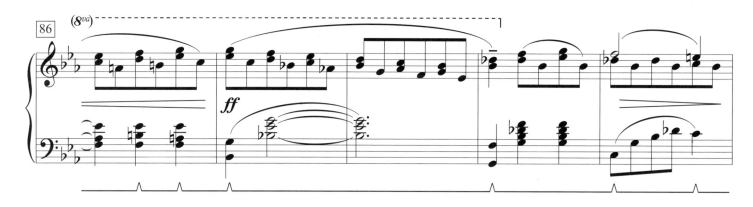

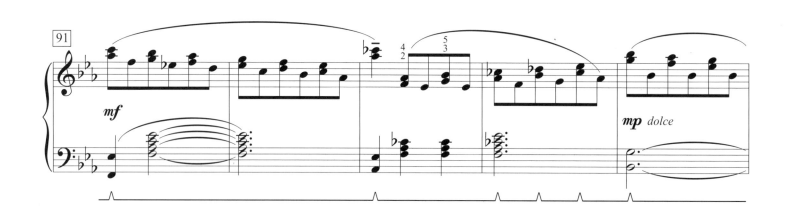

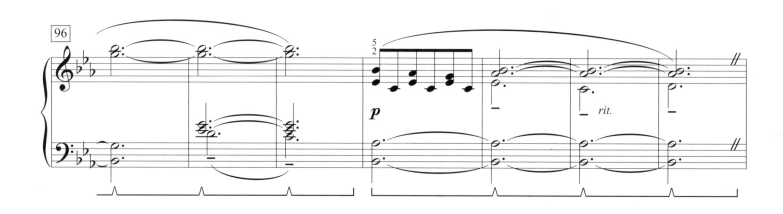

153

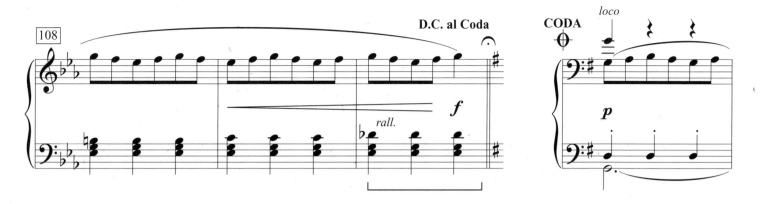

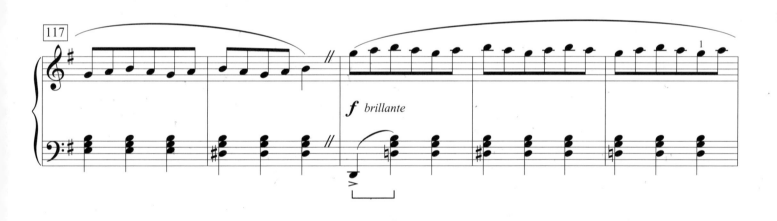

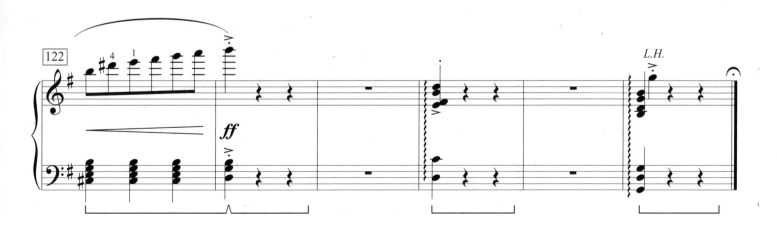

Valse Triste

William Gillock

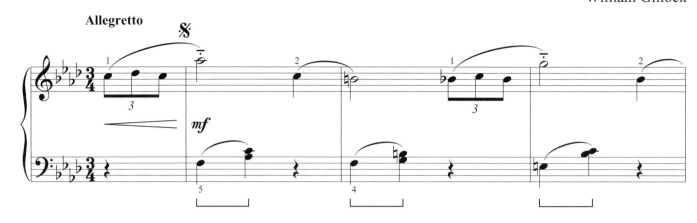

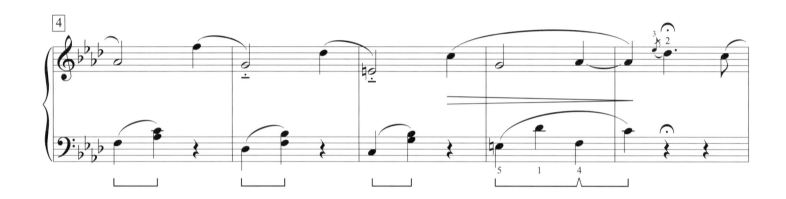

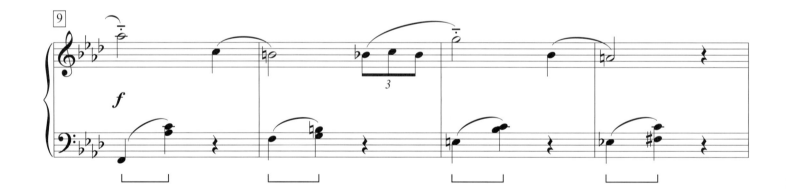

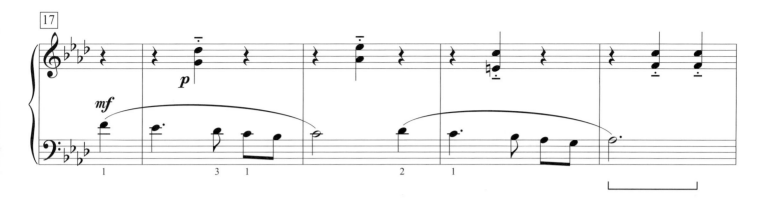

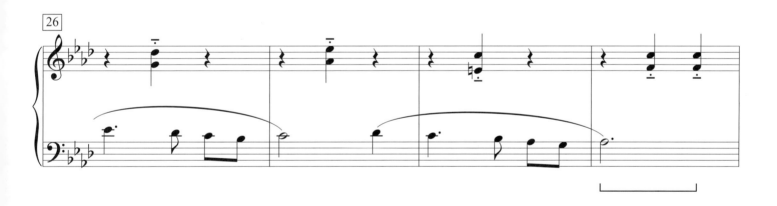

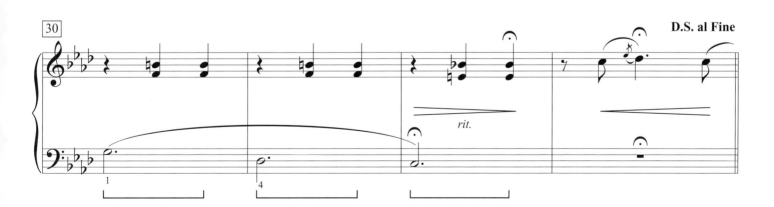

To Beverly Bradley

Viennese Rondo
(Homage to Josef Strauss)

William Gillock

NOTE: *Viennese Rondo* is also available as a piano duo (2 pianos, 4 hands).

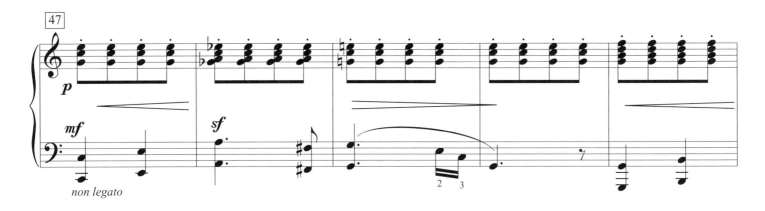

For Hiroko Yasuda

Postlude
(A Remembrance)

William Gillock

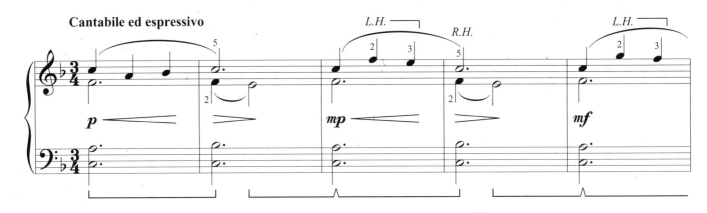

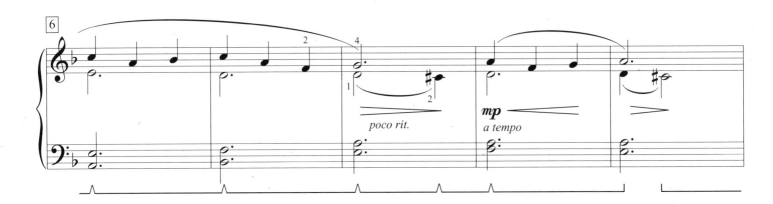

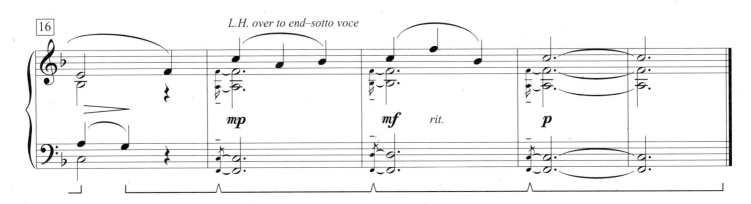